Balti

ABOUT THE AUTHOR

Lynette Baxter gained a degree in Home Economics from the University of Surrey, which led to a career in the food industry. She works on product and recipe development for major high street retailers. When she first became aware of the Balti style of cookery, she realised that it was ideal for busy cooks to create at home. She has a firm belief that anyone can cook anything armed with a good recipe and hopes that this book will encourage others to feel the same.

SPECIALITY KITCHEN

Balti

THE COMPLETE COOKBOOK

Lynette Baxter

GREENWICH EDITIONS

ACKNOWLEDGEMENTS

This edition reprinted in 1998 by Greenwich Editions,
Brewery Road, London N7 9NT

Design: Amanda Hawkes
Illustrations: Beryl Sanders
Cover photograph: Jhon Kevern
Editor: Nicola Baxter

The author and publishers wish to thank
Jane Allcorn and Adrian Reeve for their
help with this book.

ISBN 0-86288-275-3

First edition published by Blitz Editions
an imprint of Bookmart Limited
Registered Number 2372865
Trading as Bookmart Limited, Desford Road, Enderby,
Leicester, LE9 5AD, England
Reprinted 1995 (twice).

Produced for Bookmart Limited by Nicola Baxter

Printed in Great Britain

CONTENTS

WHAT IS BALTI?

ave you noticed Balti sauces and ready meals appearing in your supermarket? Seen Balti mentioned in magazine articles? Caught sight of a round, two-handled Balti pan for sale in your local cook shop? Or perhaps you're one of the many enthusiasts who have enjoyed a Balti dish at one of the Balti houses that seem to be springing up everywhere.

The Balti invasion started about 20 years ago, but unless you were living in a specific part of Birmingham at the time, you were probably totally unaware of it until quite recently. So what is Balti? To answer that question, we need to delve into a little history and geography.

Basically, Balti is a type of Kashmiri curry, originating amongst the Balti people of Baltistan (yes, there really is such a place - in northern Pakistan). After the Second World War, large numbers of Pakistanis left their homeland to begin new lives all over the world. Some came to Britain and many settled in cities in the Midlands, such as Birmingham. Gradually, small communities grew and thrived. Not surprisingly, restaurants were opened offering traditional dishes from the Indian sub-continent.

Balti houses, as Balti restaurants are often called, began to be opened in Birmingham in the 1970s. Then, as today, many of them were based on the simpler eating establishments of Northern Pakistan, in style nearer to transport cafés than more formal restaurants. The menus were fairly basic and the furnishings simple, but the food was good - and cheap. As they were owned and run by Muslims, they tended to be unlicensed, but diners could bring their own drinks with them if they wished. These restaurants gained an enthusiastic non-Asian clientele. Gradually, Balti house menus widened to include more traditional dishes, where the aromatic flavour of herbs and spices, garlic and ginger, was not overpowered by large amounts of chilli. Slowly a whole new restaurant culture started springing up all over Birmingham. Today, that story is being repeated all over the country, with many long-established Indian restaurants also offering Balti dishes.

What Is Balti?
✦✦✦

Balti cookery's origins, back in Northern Pakistan, have clear Chinese influences. Even the Balti cooking pan is closely related to the wok. But when looking for Balti's roots, it is clear that what is enjoyed in the Balti houses of Britain today is a style of cookery that has developed along its own lines in the last twenty years.

The indigenous peoples of Baltistan have traditionally lived a nomadic existence, cooking meat from their flocks or hunted game. The cooking pot, or karahi, is placed on a pile of glowing embers and any available meat and vegetables are cooked in the one dish and seasoned with dried spices. The resultant casserole is tender and fragrant, full of aromatic ingredients enhanced by a long, slow cooking.

The adaptation of Balti cooking to the British palette means that when we talk of authentic dishes, we mean an authentic Birmingham rather than an authentic Baltistani style. The modern British Balti house has retained its links with the karahi and the aromatic seasoning of dishes, but its repertoire has expanded to include many of the dishes one would expect to see in a long-established Indian restaurant. You will frequently come across such dishes as Balti Tikka Masala and Balti Rogan Josh, for example.

In some respects, one of the great joys of cooking Balti dishes at home has much in common with Balti's origins. Like the nomadic people of Baltistan, you can cook what you find available - but in the store cupboard, freezer or refrigerator, rather than wandering the plains! Balti cookery is ideal for today's busy cook. It can be adapted to what you have to hand, it is quick and easy, and it is delicious.

The best kept secret of most Balti houses is their Balti sauce or blend of spices. This can be true of your Balti cookery too, as you adapt recipes to suit your own tastes and favourite flavours. I cannot stress too often that the recipes in this book are intended as a guide - a starting point for your own ideas.

"Balti", as you may have guessed by now, is a multi-purpose word. It is used to describe not only the people of a particular region and a style of cookery but also the pan in which Balti food is cooked. This round, metal, two-handled pan comes in a variety of sizes and is one of the most immediately recognisable features of Balti. The food is cooked in the pan (also known as a karahi, as mentioned above) and often served in a smaller version of the same pan. The food is served, still sizzling, freshly cooked to retain all its aroma and flavour. The best Baltis rely on the subtle flavours of their ingredients rather than a mind-numbing heat level. Often they are based on onions and tomatoes, with cumin, coriander and fenugreek being the most popular flavours.

Traditionally, Baltis are served with bread, rather than rice, and no cutlery. Like your first experience of chopsticks, this can be something of a challenge. The idea is to break off a small piece of bread and, holding it in your right hand, use it to scoop up a mouthful of Balti. If you find that this results in you eating more bread than Balti, there's no shame in resorting to a fork!

One of the beauties of Balti is its simplicity. You can quickly master the basic recipes and cooking techniques to achieve a very authentic result. Because the flavour of Balti is characterised by the sauce and spices used, there is a certain similarity between dishes, making it ideal for the brilliant Balti idea of combining. In many Balti houses, rather in the same way that you can select your own pizza toppings in some Italian restaurants, you can choose to mix and match different dishes to make your favourite combination. Some ideas are fairly obvious - combining a meat Balti with a vegetable Balti, for example, but that is only the beginning. On the menus of Balti restaurants you will often find 50 or

60 dishes on offer. Many of these are spectacular combinations, often written in a kind of Balti shorthand. The exotic dish called Balti Mt-Aub-Chi-Spi-Mush takes on manageable proportions when you realise that this is a meat Balti with aubergines, chick peas, spinach and mushrooms. Other dishes combine meat, poultry and fish. Balti lamb, chicken and prawn is a particularly popular mix.

Despite the length of Balti menus, they will often end with a note to say that if there is any combination you would like that is not mentioned on the menu, it will be willingly prepared for you. Bear this in mind when creating your Balti dishes at home. Once you have become quite confident with the basic sauces and spice mixes, which will not take long, and have a few successful dishes behind you, you will be ready to begin adapting, mixing and matching. This is where the fun starts!

Fun is what Balti is all about. Balti meals should be fun to prepare, fun to cook and fun to eat. Preparation is easy because it can be done well in advance. Your sauces, spice mixes and pre-cooked meat and vegetables can be made early in the day, or even further in advance and frozen. Cooking is easy because once your basic preparation is done, you are just flinging ingredients one after another into the same pan. Eating is definitely fun if you follow the traditional custom of eating with bread, and, of course, because Baltis are delicious! Even clearing up is less of a chore than usual because you have only one cooking pan and no cutlery to wash up.

If you are still at all uncertain about producing your own Baltis, why not visit a Balti restaurant to get a few ideas. Although Birmingham is the homeland of Balti in this country, it is now available just about everywhere. You will probably find that even if you don't have a specialised Balti house nearby, your local Indian restaurant will offer a number of Balti dishes.

In these days when people are increasingly aware of what they eat and the overall quality of their diet, Balti has good and bad points. Probably the least healthy aspect of Balti cookery is the fact that most dishes are fried. You can improve matters by using a cooking oil high in polyunsaturates, such as sunflower oil. You may also be able to reduce the amount of oil included in the recipes if you use a non-stick frying pan or wok. On the plus side, Balti dishes are full of lean meat and vegetables. Using poultry and white fish as the basis of recipes is generally considered a healthier option than using red meat or shellfish. Where yoghurt is mentioned, you can certainly use a low fat version, and yoghurt can replace cream in some of the few recipes where it occurs. If you are trying to cut down the fat in your diet, serve your Balti with one of the plainer breads.

Nothing can disguise the fact that many of the desserts served at the end of a Balti meal are not designed with the health conscious in mind, but fruit salad or fresh mango makes a delicious finale. In fact, Balti main courses are often very substantial and any dessert may well be out of the question to all but those unrepentant souls who, like myself, read a menu backwards, planning an entire meal dessert-wards!

USING THIS
BOOK

I have already explained that one of the many great things about preparing food the Balti way is the simplicity of that preparation. Balti cookery does, however, have a few new techniques and methods and the order in which things are done is important. For that reason, I would suggest that the Balti novice takes a little time to read through at least the introductory sections of this book rather than plunging straight into a recipe. Baltis are "built" stage by stage, and the foundations must be secure.

The first part of this book forms an introduction to Balti, the equipment it requires, its most common ingredients and the techniques used. You will almost certainly find that your kitchen already contains all the equipment and most of the ingredients that you need to begin. Nor is there anything alarming or difficult about Balti cooking techniques - you will become familiar with them extremely quickly.

The main part of the book, giving Balti recipes, is divided into several sections, each beginning with a list of recipes to be covered in that section. You will find that I have usually used English names for dishes, unless there is no suitable translation. This is to help with the speedy selection of recipes - you will know that a dish is based on lamb and includes tomatoes, for example, if it says so in the title. You will find that all recipes give an estimate of the number of people they will serve and a preparation time. If the recipes include pre-prepared ingredients, such as Balti sauce, the time taken to make this is not included in the preparation time. On the other hand, you will not necessarily have to stand over the stove throughout the whole preparation time - skim through the recipe to check.

I have not included a "heat rating" in these recipes because one person's mild can bring tears to the eyes of another. Instead, I would suggest that you get to know the strength of your chilli powder, fresh chillies and ginger so that you can adapt the heat of recipes to your own taste.

At the end of many recipes you will find a "Cook's tip". This may give a technique or piece of information that I have found it useful to know when preparing that particular recipe, or suggest a variation on the main recipe for future use. I hope that you will soon find yourself scribbling in your own tips as you try the recipes and work out your own adaptations. Experimentation is the secret of all great original cooking, and Balti lends itself to this particularly well.

The recipe sections are as follows:

BALTI BASICS

In many ways, this is the most important section as these recipes are the foundations from which your Balti dishes will grow. Developing your own versions of the Balti sauce, Balti spice mix and Balti garam masala will add an individuality to your cookery.

POULTRY AND GAME

This section begins with a brief introduction to the range of poultry and game now readily available and how to prepare it. A basic Balti poultry recipe is followed by more adventurous dishes.

MEAT

Unlike poultry or fish, larger cuts of meat should be pre-cooked before being used in a Balti recipe. Instructions for doing this are followed by recipes, some very easy, others more challenging, but all delicious.

FISH AND SHELLFISH

A list of the various types of fish and shellfish available is followed by a number of recipes designed to include as wide a range of these as possible.

VEGETABLES

This section begins by introducing vegetables most frequently used in Balti dishes and explaining any pre-preparation that may be necessary before including them in a dish. The list of vegetables is by no means exhaustive - you will no doubt want to add your own favourites. The recipes that follow include side dishes and vegetarian main meals.

ACCOMPANIMENTS

Bread is the most important addition to a Balti meal, and here you will find recipes for a number of different kinds. I have also included ideas for chutneys, salads and dips to enliven your meal.

DESSERTS

This section includes some of the most popular Indian and Pakistani desserts, any of which would make the perfect ending to a Balti meal.

DRINKS

What should be drunk with a Balti dish is certainly open to debate, but the recipes in this section will perhaps give you some fresh ideas.

A BALTI BANQUET

After a while you will probably want to impress your friends with your Balti cookery skills. Entertaining with Balti can be delightful. Here you will find ideas for an evening of serious eating: pre-dinner nibbles, starters, special main courses and variations on dessert themes. There are also suggestions for party menus.

CURRY IN A HURRY

Balti cooking is rarely a time-consuming business, but today's busy lifestyles leave little leisure for meal preparation. Here I offer some tips for speeding up your Balti cooking without detracting from its quality and flavour.

USEFUL INFORMATION

At the end of the book you will find lists and indexes to help you make the most of this book and increase your enjoyment of Balti cookery. These include:

◆ Addresses that may prove useful if you are having difficulty in sourcing any of the ingredients or equipment mentioned.

◆ A Glossary, listing some of the traditional names for ingredients and dishes and their English equivalents. This may be useful if you find yourself in a specialist shop or interpreting the menu in a Balti restaurant. And when your guests demand to know the secret ingredients of the dish they have just eaten, you can mystify them further by murmuring about methi, gosht and murghi!

◆ A general Index containing recipes, ingredients and topics that have been covered in the introductory sections throughout the book.

I hope that you will enjoy cooking the recipes in this book as much as I have enjoyed researching, developing and - most important of all - eating them.

BALTI COOKING
AT HOME

Balti is certainly one of the fastest growing trends in cookery today, but unlike many new fads, it is not difficult or expensive to join in. The equipment required is very little different from that found in almost every kitchen, and apart from a few spices, the ingredients used are not particularly exotic. You will find most of them already on your store cupboard shelves.

On the following pages I have outlined briefly the equipment you will need for cooking the Balti recipes in this book. The specialist items mentioned may make life easier or your presentation of finished dishes more interesting, but they are not essential. That would be going against the spirit of Balti. After all, nomadic people do not burden themselves with an enormous *batterie de cuisine* when they are on the move! Armed with a sharp knife, a frying pan and a wooden spoon, you could tackle most of the recipes in this book.

I must confess that I am not a great gadget fan. It always seems quicker to me to crush a clove of garlic with the flat side of a knife than to use and wash up a garlic crusher, but I know that not everyone feels this way, so I have mentioned some electrical equipment you might like to consider.

I have also included some ideas on storing and freezing Balti dishes. In an ideal world, Baltis are served fresh and sizzling, straight from the pan, but in the real world, cooks get delayed at work and guests cancel at the last minute, so it is always useful to have a freezing option.

Finally, I have given some ideas on Balti presentation, which is half the fun of this food phenomenon.

BALTI PANS

The Balti pan, or karahi, is probably the only piece of equipment for making Baltis that is not already in your kitchen. They are now quite easily available and not expensive in Asian stores and good cook shops. Usually they are made of stainless steel, but you may also find the more traditional, blackened cast-iron pans. Balti pans come in a range of sizes, for cooking main courses and side dishes and for serving.

It is the serving-sized dishes, complete with stands, that are most readily available. Always buy the stand, or invest in some very thick cork mats, because Baltis should be served sizzling hot and can easily damage woodwork! If you can only invest in one new item, a set of serving dishes and stands would be my choice, particularly if you are planning to entertain with Balti. The alternative - serving on a plate - rather spoils the authentic look of your cooking, although, of course, the Balti will taste just as delicious.

A Balti cooking pan is a luxury that you can easily manage without. A wok or a reasonably large frying pan will suffice for the recipes in this book. A wok is particularly useful if you are catering for large numbers. An electric frying pan would also work successfully.

If you buy a new Balti pan, or indeed wok, to cook in, you will need to season it. This means that you start to build up a protective layer on your pan, which over time becomes a kind of do-it-yourself non-stick finish. First of all, thoroughly clean the new pan with a mild cleaner, then rinse and dry it well. Put about 60ml (4tbspn) of vegetable oil in the pan and heat it to smoking point on top of the oven. Carefully swirl the oil around the pan to cover as much of the sides as possible, but do watch out that there's no danger of it spattering over the edge. Turn off the heat and allow the pan and oil to cool. Then discard the oil and wipe out the pan with kitchen paper.

When you have begun cooking in your pan, you should be able to clean it after use simply by wiping carefully with kitchen paper again. Scourers and washing up liquid will destroy the build-up of oil you've achieved. Persistently stuck-on food should respond to a soak in warm water, but if you stir frequently as suggested in the recipes, this should not be a problem.

BALTI PAN EXTRAS

If you own a wok, you will probably find that it came complete with a lid, stand and several wooden tools. Don't hesitate to hi-jack this equipment for your Balti cookery. If not, you will need the lid of your largest saucepan. If this is still not large enough to cover your Balti or frying pan, and the recipe calls for the dish to be covered during cooking, you can use a double thickness of foil, slightly larger than the top of the pan. A thick wooden chopping board can take the place of a stand, and a good selection of wooden spoons, aided by a large wooden spatula, will be all you need for the stir-frying technique on which Balti is based.

OTHER BASIC KITCHEN EQUIPMENT

Other than the Balti pan, which is itself optional, the recipes in this book do not require any specialist equipment, but below I have provided a "checklist" of common kitchen tools that will make your Balti cookery easier and are probably already in your cupboards.

♦ A selection of knives

♦ Chopping boards: in the interests of safety and hygiene, you should ideally have at least three: one for cooked meat, one for raw meat and one for vegetables. Modern plastic chopping boards with different coloured handles make it easy to keep these separate.

◆ A range of mixing bowls, including at least one non-metallic one for marinating

◆ A range of lidded saucepans

◆ A heavy based frying pan

◆ A slotted spoon

◆ A sieve, ideally metal. If your sieve is plastic, you may have to allow ingredients to cool before sieving.

◆ Cooling racks

◆ Baking trays

◆ A grill pan and rack

◆ A deep-fat fryer. You may have a chip pan or an electric deep-fat fryer. If not, any deep pan may be used to deep fry, but obviously those designed for the purpose are safer.

COFFEE GRINDER

Apart from its normal use, this is certainly a wonderful tool if you plan to grind your own spices - a quick whiz saves several minutes of bashing with a pestle and mortar! A coffee grinder works well for dry ingredients, but don't be tempted to add "wet" items, such as garlic or fresh ginger. The juices can leak into the motor of the machine with disastrous consequences. For similar reasons, it is unwise to attempt to wash up the body of the grinder. A thorough wipe with kitchen paper should be enough. Remember to be particularly thorough in cleaning out the grinder if you have last used it to mill coffee beans. A faintly spicy flavour to your coffee can be quite pleasant, but a coffee-flavoured Balti is not a happy thought!

FOOD PROCESSOR

Several times in the recipes that follow you will see that I have suggested how the preparation can be speeded up by the use of a food processor. In most cases, a liquidiser is equally successful. If you already own a processor, you'll wonder how you ever managed without one. Their only real drawback is the space they take up. You will find yourself using one much more frequently if you have space to keep it standing on your worktop - then you only have to find storage room for the many attachments! Of course, if you have neither a food processor nor a liquidiser, there is always another way of tackling the recipe using basic tools and a little more elbow grease.

PESTLE AND MORTAR

Using a pestle and mortar is a harder way to grind spices but very satisfying as you will be able to savour the aroma as you crush the seeds. You can also use it to make pastes from crushed garlic cloves, grated ginger, chopped onion and chopped green chillies. Grinding down ingredients in this way will actually give you a smoother sauce with a more even distribution of flavours than mechanical methods. In fact you may find that you will need to reduce the amount of chilli you use.

MICROWAVE OVEN

Cooks' opinions of microwaves vary from those who wouldn't be without one to those who wouldn't even consider letting one into their kitchen. I have never been one of those microwave fans who claim that they use it to cook everything including the Sunday roast. On the other hand, I do find it an extremely useful gadget. It is excellent for softening hard fats, melting chocolate and jellies and making custards and sauces. In Balti cookery it can blanch vegetables, defrost frozen stocks and sauces, warm up pre-prepared meals and even produce a very creditably crispy poppadom!

Microwave ovens effect ingredients in a similar way to steaming. They do not crisp up food (apart from poppadoms) and are not ideal for heating breads or anything deep-fried that is designed to be crisp.

There is now a huge range of microwave ovens on the market, including many that incorporate grills and combination ovens. They can range in power output, with something between 600 and 850 Watts being the output of most domestic models. They also vary greatly in price and size. If you are considering buying a microwave, or updating your old one, do think carefully about what you actually intend to use it for. There's little point in spending hundreds of pounds on an all-singing, all-dancing model if you only want it to heat your bedtime cocoa.

STORING BALTIS

Balti dishes are stir fries and as such should be cooked and then served as quickly as possible. That doesn't mean that anything that isn't eaten has to be thrown away. Most Balti dishes will store and reheat quite successfully, but like all food should be handled carefully and sensibly. Any leftover Balti should be cooled as quickly as possible, then covered and stored in the refrigerator. It should be eaten within two days, having first been thoroughly reheated. The texture and flavour of a Balti may change slightly during storage and reheating. Vegetables will tend to soften, meat may lose some of its texture, and flavours may weaken. Sauces sometimes disappear - they seem to be absorbed by the food - so you may need to add a little more liquid when reheating.

You can, of course, adapt a recipe slightly if you know that you will be reheating the dish, rather than eating it straight away. In this case you can undercook the vegetables and add a little more sauce than usual. Seasonings and flavours are more difficult to adjust. Although some may weaken, I always find that a chilli left in the refrigerator seems far more fiery the next day.

Balti sauce keeps in the refrigerator for up to a week, while par-cooked meat can be stored for two days.

You may be happier to store leftover food in the freezer. Basically, the same rules apply. Although most Baltis freeze very successfully, you may find that those with a high proportion of vegetables become rather "mushy". However, the freezer has many other uses for the Balti cook. Here are some suggestions:

◆ Make a huge batch of Balti sauce and freeze it in convenient portions: 150-275ml ($^1/_4$-$^1/_2$pt) is usually ideal. Clean margarine tubs are useful for this.

◆ Pre-cook batches of dried lentils, beans and peas. It is just as quick to cook 20 portions as it is to cook two. Cool down quickly after cooking and divide into 225g (8oz) portions, or to suit your own needs. It's better to err on the small side. You can always take out two packs when you need them, but chiselling a frozen lump of chick peas in half is hard work!

◆ Batch par-cook meat and freeze it in 450-560g (1-1$^1/_4$lb) packs. You can freeze whole pieces or dice them before freezing.

◆ If you grow your own vegetables, you probably already freeze them when you have a glut, but it is also worth raiding your local freezer centre or supermarket for special offers. Some vegetables freeze

extremely well and are always worth keeping in store. These include sweetcorn, green beans, spinach (chopped or whole leaf) and, of course, peas.

◆ Small amounts of crushed garlic, chopped green chilli and grated fresh ginger can be frozen. I find that the best way is to press the prepared ingredient into an ice-cube tray. You can then pop them out when frozen and store them in plastic bags. I would strongly suggest that you use an ice-cube tray kept only for this purpose - a chilli and garlic flavoured ice cube floating in a martini is unlikely to be well received!

◆ Commercially produced naan bread freezes well. In fact, it is available, ready frozen, in some supermarkets. If you make your own breads, you can also freeze them. It is best to layer grease proof paper or foil between each piece of bread, or they may stick together. But don't use foil if you intend to defrost them in a microwave.

Freezing food requires only common sense, but you may wish to bear the following points in mind:

◆ Freezing delays the spoilage of food that is caused by bacteria but it doesn't destroy the bugs - it just makes them very sleepy. Only freeze food that is fresh and in tip-top condition, and use it within 3 months of freezing to get best results.

◆ Food that has a high water content is not generally a successful candidate for freezing. Vegetables such as marrow and cucumber do not freeze successfully. Freezing causes the water to expand as it cools and this ruptures the cells of the vegetable, resulting in a mushy effect when defrosted. As a rule, commercially frozen products are better because they have been frozen so quickly, while domestic freezers are less efficient and can take several hours to freeze solid.

◆ If you know that a dish is going to be frozen, slightly undercook it. This allows for the softening effect of freezing and the additional reheating time.

◆ Freeze the dish as soon as it is cooked and cooled, but don't put warm food in the freezer as it will raise the cabinet temperature and put other frozen foods at risk.

◆ Always label dishes and ingredients you put in the freezer with both a name and a date. It may be obvious to you what they are when you put a bag of cooked lentils into the freezer, but three months later they can easily be mistaken for apple purée.

◆ Even in the freezer, spicy foods can taint other dishes, so always make sure that the containers you use are well sealed.

◆ You may need to adjust the seasoning of dishes after they have been frozen and reheated, so always taste before your serve.

◆ For safety's sake, always ensure that the dish is piping hot all the way through when you reheat it, and never defrost a frozen meal and then refreeze it.

SERVING BALTI

As I have said before, the ideal way to serve Balti is to present a sizzling karahi to each diner. It really is worth investing in these if you intend to cook Balti often. They will also double as serving dishes for other kinds of curry.

The Balti table is quite simple. Each place should have a stand for a Balti pan, ideally standing on a thick place mat. Because cutlery is not used, there is no need for formal table laying, but a finger bowl for each diner, with a fresh flower floating in it, is a nice touch. Certainly plenty of napkins are required but this is probably not the time to bring out your best white damask - turmeric is notoriously difficult to wash out.

A large basket is ideal for serving bread. You could offer side plates for the bread, or it can be laid directly on the table. If scooping up food with bread is new to your guests, you may like to supply a fork or dessertspoon. You can munch your way through a great deal of bread scooping up a dish of Balti. It would be a shame if diners couldn't do justice to the main dish because they were full of the accompaniment.

It is nice to have a choice of chutneys to go with the meal and perhaps a cooling dish of raita or a salad. These look particularly attractive if served in small Balti dishes.

Portion sizes depend on the appetites of your fellow-eaters and what else you are serving. Eating Balti is a very sociable event - people tend to linger over their meals and may eat more than they would normally. The recipes in this book give the number of servings, but as a rough guide, you should allow about 150-175g (5-6oz) of uncooked protein per person.

If you are unsure of your guests' tastes, it is kinder to start with a mild Balti dish or at least to offer a choice. If you find yourself with a table of diners visibly perspiring and ready to drink the contents of their finger bowls, you have probably over-done the chilli level!

BALTI
INGREDIENTS

any of the ingredients used in Balti cookery would once have been described as specialist but today can be found on most supermarket shelves. The rise in popularity of foods from all over the world has meant that shops have had to respond to the demand for new ingredients. On the whole, you should have few problems in tracking down any of the ingredients mentioned in this book. In case a few do evade you, however, or if you live in a very remote area, you will find addresses of mail-order suppliers at the end of the book.

The biggest and perhaps the most important range of ingredients is the spices. A few are essentials in nearly all recipes, while others crop up occasionally. In this section you will find information on how best to buy, store and process your spices. Spices are at the heart of Balti cookery and their subtle blending will give each dish its own character.

Oils and fats are also important because Baltis are almost always fried. The quality of oil used will affect the end result of the dish, so you need to choose carefully from the vast range available.

Other slightly unusual ingredients that you will encounter include gram flour, coconut milk, root ginger and fresh coriander. If these are not readily available, it is sometimes possible to substitute another ingredient. In the following pages you will find advice on this.

As you become expert in Balti cookery, you will find that your store cupboard will expand to include an exciting range of herbs, spices and ingredients. The following pages will help you to become familiar with them before this happens.

SPICES

As I have mentioned, these are the ingredients that will shape your Balti cookery. It is important that you treat them in a way that brings out the best of their wonderful flavours and pungent aromas.

Ideally spices should be bought whole and roasted and ground in your kitchen. This may sound like a counsel of perfection, but the first time you smell freshly roasted and ground spices you will realise what you have been missing. Of course, you can buy ready ground spices but you should be aware that they have a limited shelf-life. Tests have shown that their pungency drops noticeably after about three months. However, they are now well packaged, often sealed in small sachets or air-tight jars, and freshly bought they are an acceptable alternative to freshly ground spices. In fact, one or two spices are actually too fibrous to be ground successfully at home. Turmeric and ginger are good examples of this.

If you are roasting and grinding your own spices, you can be sure of two things. Firstly, you will know exactly how fresh your spices are, and secondly, you will know exactly what has gone into your ground spice. This means that you can be confident that it does not contain stalks and other rubbish, or inferior quality spices. Another advantage is that very few factory-ground spices are roasted first, so your spices will have a superior flavour. And when it comes to making spice blends, such as garam masala, you will be able to make the mix exactly to your own requirements.

ROASTING AND GRINDING SPICES

Roasting is not really an accurate description of what you will be doing to spices. In fact, you will be heating them to release their essential oils. This will take the raw edge off the flavour of the spice and fill your kitchen with wonderful aromas.

The easiest way to "roast" spices is to put them in a small saucepan over a medium heat for a few minutes, shaking the pan gently until you smell the aroma and a little steam is given off. Be careful not to scorch the spices, as this will give them a bitter flavour. If you do cook the spices too fiercely at your first attempt, it is better to throw them away. Trying to use them could mean that you spoil a whole recipe, rather than just a few spices.

Allow the roast spices to cool before whizzing them in a coffee grinder or pounding them with a pestle and mortar. You can roast and grind spices individually or cook and grind them together if you are making a blend. Any mix of two or more spices is a blend or "masala", and it is these different blends that distinguish the recipes.

On the following pages you will find more detailed information about different spices, divided into those that you can buy whole and roast yourself and those that it is better to buy ready ground. Those marked with an asterisk are essential spices that you will need to have to hand before you begin your first Balti dish. The others you can gradually acquire later.

The one thing that many ground spices have in common is their brownish, powdery appearance. Always label your spices carefully with their name and date of grinding. Store them in fairly small amounts in airtight jars in a cool, dark cupboard. If you find that you have roasted and ground too large a quantity, give some spices away to friends - they will be delighted, and it is much better than having a cupboard full of old and increasingly flavourless spices.

Balti Ingredients
♦♦♦

SPICES TO BUY WHOLE

Bay leaves*

Cardamom pods

Cassia or cinnamon

Red and green chillies

Cloves

Coriander seeds*

Cumin seeds*

Fennel seeds*

Dried fenugreek leaves*

Mustard seeds

Black peppercorns

Sesame seeds

SPICES TO BUY READY GROUND

Black pepper

Chilli powder*

Coriander (acceptable if you don't want to grind your own)

Cumin (as coriander)

Ginger*

Paprika*

Star anise

Turmeric*

BAY LEAVES

These dark aromatic leaves are from a tree grown world-wide. In fact, you may have one yourself in the garden or in a pot on the windowsill, in which case supplies should be no problem. Imported bay leaves usually come from Turkey and fresh stocks become available in this country around November. Bay leaves can be infused whole or ground and used in spice mixes. They are used in Balti cookery as a successful replacement for the cassia tree leaf, unobtainable outside the Indian sub-continent.

CARDAMOM PODS

There are three types of cardamom pods:

Black or brown ones have dark, slightly hairy cases and a pungent flavour. They are usually added to pullao rice and are not usually intended to be eaten.

Green ones have a smooth, green outer casing, about 1cm ($^1/_2$ inch) long, housing small black seeds. They can be used whole, often lightly bruised to release more of the flavour, or the seeds can be ground. Removing the seeds is rather a fiddly process, but they are not often sold out of their pods as they lose their flavour and aroma very quickly. If the recipe calls for ground cardamom seeds, use a pestle and mortar to grind them - the amounts will be so small that you may lose them in a grinder.

White ones are similar to green but the outer casing is paler because they have been bleached. As a result, the flavour and aroma is slightly inferior to that of the green ones. However, it is white cardamom pods that are most readily available in supermarkets and where a recipe calls for cardamom pods, either white or green can be used. The cardamom on sale in Britain usually comes from India or Sri Lanka and will be at its freshest from December to January.

CASSIA OR CINNAMON

Cassia is the corky outer bark of a tree originating in China and Indonesia. It has a fragrance very similar to cinnamon and the two are often confused. Cassia is thicker and tougher than cinnamon and can therefore stand up to more vigorous cooking methods. Its aromatic flavour enhances meat and poultry dishes as well as rice, but it should not itself be eaten.

Cinnamon is the finer inner bark of a tree originally found in China. Nowadays most of our supplies come from the Seychelles and Madagascar. It is usually sold in a rolled stick, looking a little like a loosely rolled cigar. Cinnamon sticks may be up to 1cm ($1/2$ inch) in diameter and 10-20cm (4-8 inches) long. Because they are quite fragile and break up easily when cooked, cinnamon sticks are usually used for infusing and then removed. Ground cinnamon can be used in some recipes.

RED AND GREEN CHILLIES

There are many species of chilli and even within species the heat can vary greatly. All chillies start off green and ripen to red, but they can be long and thin or quite stubby and fat. They can be bought fresh or dried. The dried variety are about 4-5cm ($1^1/2$-2 inches) long and about 1cm ($1/2$ inch) in diameter. They may be used on their own, when they are often fried in hot oil to release their flavour, or in a spice mix. If you want the flavour of chillies without the heat, simply cut off the stalk end and shake out and discard the seeds. If you are using fresh chillies, trim off the stalk end and cut into rings, or chop into small pieces. You can scrape out the seeds, but it is usual to include them in recipes. People vary too in the amount of heat they like or can tolerate, so start modestly - you can always add more. Remember, however, that other ingredients of the Balti, such as ginger and chilli powder, will also contribute heat, and it would be a shame to mask the other flavours. Unless you are feeding a rugby team, be cautious with chillies!

Finally, do handle chillies carefully when you are cooking and wash your hands thoroughly after touching them. The tiniest trace on your fiingers can irritate and burn sensitive skin. If you rub your eyes while handling chillies, be sure to flush them out with plenty of cold water to reduce the painful irritation that will result. Be careful, too, if you need to interrupt your cooking to tend to a small child, whose skin will be even more sensitive than your own. And before I leave the subject, male cooks have begged me to mention that this is a case where washing hands before taking a natural break is as important as washing them afterwards!

CLOVES

Most cloves come from Indonesia, Malaysia, Zanzibar and Madagascar. They will be at their freshest in February and March. This is one spice that you should have no difficulty in obtaining. Brought to Britain by the Romans, it has long been an essential ingredient of traditional apple pies. As any toothache sufferer will know, cloves contain a pain-killing essential oil. The cloves that we use are actually the unopened buds of a tree from the myrtle family. They start off bright green and are picked when they become pink. On drying, they turn a darkish red/brown. Cloves may be used whole in dishes, in which case they are not eaten, or ground and used in spice mixes.

CORIANDER SEEDS, WHOLE AND GROUND

Coriander seeds are small, round and beige. They are imported from India, Egypt and Morocco and are one of the most essential spices for Balti cookery. Although the seeds are a similar size and shape to peppercorns, they are much more delicate and are easily crushed to a powder. You can use the ready ground variety, but it is very easy to grind the whole seeds at home. Coriander loses its pungency quite quickly, after which it tastes like sawdust, so be ruthless about throwing out old stocks and replacing with fresh. With a spice so crucial to your Balti cuisine, it is pointless to risk using sub-standard stocks.

CUMIN SEEDS, WHOLE AND GROUND

Cumin seeds resemble caraway seeds in appearance but have a wonderfully warm and rounded spicy aroma and flavour. They can enhance your Balti recipes in a number of ways. The seeds can be roasted and ground and incorporated into nearly every Balti recipe. Cumin can easily be bought ready ground, but its wonderful flavour and aroma is delicate and volatile, so home-produced supplies will certainly be superior. Cumin seeds can also be thrown into the hot oil in the first stage of a Balti dish's preparation, acting as both a flavour and a garnish. Black cumin seeds are, as their name suggests, darker than the more common white variety, and also thinner and smaller. Black cumin is only used whole, generally in rice and vegetable dishes. It is usually eaten with the dish, to which it imparts an almost nutty flavour. Most cumin comes from India, Iran and Turkey, with fresh stocks arriving from late summer to early autumn.

FENNEL SEEDS

These are pale green, slightly striped seeds, similar to, but slightly larger than, cumin seeds. People either love or loathe fennel, depending on whether they like aniseed. Although the flavour is mild, there is a distinct anise taste, which adds a sweet, aromatic warmth to Balti dishes. Roasted fennel seeds can also be offered at the end of a meal as a mouth freshener and digestive.

DRIED FENUGREEK LEAVES

Here is another Balti essential. Fenugreek is available in two forms, seeds and leaves, but it is the crushed dried leaves that add authenticity to a Balti dish. They are specifically mentioned in some recipes in this book, but can be added to almost any Balti. They have a pungent and savoury flavour, so be cautious. Adding too much can leave a bitter taste. I have specified dried fenugreek leaves because you will be extremely lucky to find fresh ones. Fenugreek is imported from India and Morocco and is the one basic Balti ingredient that I have ever experienced real difficulty in finding. The answer is to stock up when you do find a source. As a dried herb, rather than a true spice, they have a slightly longer shelf life. Fenugreek seeds are quite bitter but can be included, in moderation, in spice blends. Roasting them rounds out the flavour and gives it depth. Use this spice in small quantities until you are sure of its flavour and qualities.

MUSTARD SEEDS

Whether black or white, mustard seeds have little in common with the bright yellow powder or paste we generally call mustard. The seeds are small and round and have a bitter and unappetising flavour when raw but once roasted become sweet and less pungent. They are, in fact, not as hot as you might expect. If you have not used mustard seeds before, then you are in for a treat. Try dropping the seeds into hot oil, where they will become deliciously nutty. They are quite often paired with cumin seeds and sizzled together in hot oil for a few seconds at the beginning of a Balti recipe. Unless your pan is very deep, it is wise to cover it at this stage, as the seeds are inclined to pop everywhere and may be found in the corners of your kitchen days later! Most of our stocks are either home grown or imported from Canada.

BLACK PEPPERCORNS, WHOLE AND GROUND

Pepper is another of the spices we are indebted to the Romans for introducing to this country. Peppercorns are the fruit of the pepper vine and grow in long clusters. They start green and gradually mature through yellow to crimson when fully ripe. Black peppercorns are obtained when the leaves start to turn yellow. They are dried in the sun and within a day or two become the black and shrivelled peppercorns we are familiar with. Since the pepper vine only grows in monsoon forests, most peppercorns are imported from Brazil, Indonesia, India and Malaysia. Peppercorns may be used whole, or in spice blends. They can be bought ready ground but are at their most aromatic bought whole and freshly ground on to food just prior to eating. Black pepper adds a delicate pungency to yoghurt-based dishes and raitas. It is particularly good freshly ground on to a savoury lassi (yoghurt drink, see page 202).

SESAME SEEDS

These are tiny white, tear-drop shaped seeds, mostly imported from North and Central America. The whitest and shiniest seeds have had the outer husks removed, while the browner, duller seeds are intact. Although not as strongly flavoured as many spices, sesame seeds provide texture and garnish as well as a delicate nutty taste all their own. Try adding sesame seeds to your naan bread mix, or sprinkle them on vegetable side dishes just before serving.

CHILLI POWDER

This is an enormously important spice in Balti cookery because it can change the nature of a dish so readily. There are literally hundreds of types of chillies, the fleshy pods of the capsicum family. Depending on which particular chilli is dried and ground, the heat level of your chilli powder can vary hugely. Chilli is said to be the hottest flavour on earth, and since chilli powder is ground from the whole chilli, including the seeds where the flavour is most intense, it can be extraordinarily hot.

Chillies were not discovered until the fifteenth century. Before this, black pepper was used to give heat in recipes. Since its discovery, chilli has, as it were, gone from strength to strength, particularly in Indian cuisine. You can grind your own powder from dried red chillies, but it is such an irritant that I would always buy my chilli powder ready ground.

The problem of achieving a consistent flavour with chilli is a tricky one. Heat levels can vary, depending on where the chillies are grown, and with India, Pakistan, China and the United States all supplying Britain's chillies, even commercial blenders have a difficult job in making a consistent mix. My solution would be to try several different brands and, when you find one that you like, stick to it. I would suggest that you avoid those labelled "mild". These are often mixed with other ingredients and can lack flavour. It is better to buy a reasonably strong and full-bodied chilli and use it sparingly. You will probably find that if you become a regular Balti eater, your tolerance of chilli will increase and you will find that you are using more in your recipes. Remember to readjust if you have guests who are less practised!

GINGER

You will find ginger used in two ways in Balti recipes. Some dishes require fresh root ginger, while others call for ground ginger. Root ginger is knobbly looking and fawn coloured. It is actually a rhizome rather than a root. You should be able to find this ingredient at your greengrocer's or in the fruit and vegetable section of your supermarket. The flesh inside is yellow and quite fibrous in texture. Some books advocate peeling it, but I feel that this is rarely necessary. Simply break off a piece the size you require, trim off any hard or dry patches and grate. You will probably be left with a fibrous pulp that will not go through the grater - discard this. I find that root ginger keeps well in a cool place or refrigerator, loosely wrapped in foil or grease proof paper. Only grate the amount you need at one time, usually described in recipes in terms of a cube of fresh root ginger of a certain size. Of course, ginger is knobbly, not square, so simply use a piece of approximately the right size. Once it is grated, ginger quickly loses its volatile flavour, so use it straight away. When you are calculating the heat of a dish, remember that ginger contributes a punch of its own.

Although this will not help with your Balti cookery, you may like to know that a piece of root ginger that you are unable to use but which has small greenish or whitish shoots beginning to form can be planted in a pot and grown as an attractive plant for your windowsill.

Ground ginger is simply the root, dried and powdered. It is the same ingredient that you would use in baking, so it is readily available. The fibrous nature of the ginger root and its toughness when it is dried makes this an unsuitable candidate for grinding yourself.

PAPRIKA

Most of the paprika we use is grown in Central Europe and Spain. In fact, it is the Hungarian word for pepper. Like chilli and cayenne, it is the ground seeds of a member of the capsicum family but is much milder. It is only available in its ground form and is generally used to add a rich red colour to dishes. Because it is relatively mild, you can afford to be a little more generous with this spice, but be warned - there is a scale of heat amongst paprikas and some suppliers blend chilli with it, so check labels carefully. As a garnish, paprika can be sprinkled over raita or other pale, yoghurt-based dishes.

STAR ANISE

Star anise is a most unusual spice, the fruit of a small tree native to China, Indo-China and Japan. The star-shaped fruit has between six and nine points radiating from its centre. These are in fact pods, each containing a shiny brown seed. Star anise is available whole or ground to a reddish brown powder. It is an extremely pungent spice and should be used sparingly as it can have quite a harsh aniseed flavour. If you dislike the flavour of aniseed, you may omit this spice from the recipes.

TURMERIC

This is also a rhizome, related to ginger. Most people will be familiar with this bright yellow spice as it is what gives piccalilli its traditional colour. Always bought ground, turmeric is readily available. Its greatest feature is its colouring property. It has a delicate taste, which can become bitter if too much is added, so use sparingly. My best advice when using turmeric is to handle it carefully, not because it is hot or an irritant like chilli, but because it stains anything with which it comes into contact. White plastic or wooden worktops and utensils will take on a yellowish tinge. Remember this too when eating a dish containing turmeric - it may not be the best meal to enjoy in front of the television on your prized cream upholstery.

FATS AND OILS

These play a very important part in Balti cookery. You may have visions of those meals served in some Indian restaurants that appear to be swimming in oil. This is unattractive, unappetising and unhealthy. There is no need to use excessive amounts of oil. To be fair, cooking methods often mean that the oil separates from the spices at the end of the cooking, but in this case it is easy to spoon away any excess or blot it up with a piece of kitchen paper.

If you visit the oil section of your local supermarket, you may be amazed at the choice of oils available. Sesame oil, grape seed oil, hazelnut or walnut oil and scores of different olive oils are just a few of those you will find displayed. Choose an oil that is labelled as low in saturates and high in polyunsaturates, as this is widely considered to be a healthier option.

In most of the recipes in this book, you will find that you may use vegetable oil or ghee. Ghee is the more authentic option, made by clarifying butter. You will find a recipe for it on page 52. The advantage of using ghee is that it can be heated to very high temperatures without burning and is therefore useful for browning onions or sizzling spices at the beginning of a recipe. However, if you prefer to use unsaturated fats and oils, you will not usually notice the difference in the finished dish. The one exception to this is when making bread. Ghee imparts a delicious, rich flavour that other fats and oils simply cannot match. You should be able to buy ghee ready made in specialist shops and larger supermarkets.

NUTS

Several recipes in this book contain nuts, both as garnish and to add texture to dishes. Most Indian desserts use nuts, usually almonds or pistachios, chopped or ground. Flaked almonds are good for sprinkling on dishes just before serving to add a lovely, crunchy texture. For this, toasted almonds are best as they retain their crispness. You can buy flaked almonds ready toasted or grill or bake them yourself. Experiment with different nuts. You will be surprised how their flavours and textures alter a dish. Unsalted peanuts and cashews, hazelnuts, almonds, pistachios, walnuts and brazil nuts can all be used.

COCONUT

You will find that coconut occurs in several different guises in Balti cookery. Desiccated coconut, creamed coconut and coconut milk all have their place and it is important to know how to use them. Nothing is better than using freshly grated coconut and it is worth trying at least once to see whether you feel that the effort is worth it.

To prepare fresh coconut, first check that your coconut will be suitable by shaking it to ensure that it is full of liquid. At one end of the coconut you will find three "eyes". Make a hole in two of these (they are fairly soft) using a screwdriver or nail. Drain off the liquid. It is said to be a refreshing drink in its own right, but I think you have to like coconut a lot for this to be so! (This liquid, although sometimes referred to as "milk", is not the same as coconut milk sometimes needed in recipes. See below.) Next crack the coconut with a hammer. Putting it into a strong plastic bag first will prevent the shattered pieces from flying everywhere. You will find that the coconut is made up of three parts: the outer husk and thick hard shell, the inner husk that clings to the flesh, and the flesh itself. The outer shell should break away easily. Next cut the flesh into manageable chunks and pare away the inner husk using a sharp knife or vegetable peeler. Rinse the white flesh and pat dry on kitchen paper before grating it. This is a rather long job using a grater or a very quick one with a food processor. The resulting grated coconut flesh will be delicious. It can be used as it is, or steeped in just enough boiling water to cover it for several hours and strained to give coconut milk for use in recipes. Delicious as this is, you may be glad to know that there are easier alternatives.

Desiccated coconut is available natural and sweetened. Always use the natural variety. It can be used dry, or moistened with a little water. It, too, can be steeped in boiling water for several hours and then strained to give coconut milk.

Creamed coconut comes in blocks, looking rather like a large cake of soap. It is a combination of finely grated coconut flesh and coconut oil, which sets solid. It should be kept under refrigeration as it can start to separate if it gets warm, with the risk of the oil becoming rancid. To use, simply cut off the size of piece you require and mix it with a little boiling water to give a smooth paste. Do not try to use it directly from the block as it will almost certainly burn.

Coconut milk is rich and creamy and available in cans, ready to use. If you do not require all the milk at once, it can be decanted into a plastic container and stored in the refrigerator for up to two weeks.

Coconut milk powder is a fairly recent introduction, of which I am already a great fan. It should be available in most large supermarkets, either with other packaged nuts, or in the exotic foods section. It does not have to be refrigerated and has an excellent shelf-life. A further advantage is that you can make up exactly the amount of milk you require. The dry powder is actually very finely ground dried coconut flesh, so you can be sure that you will get a good flavour and something of the coconut's texture.

FLOURS

If you decide to make your own breads to accompany your Baltis, you will need a range of flours. In Baltistan a special chappati flour is used, milled from hard grains of wheat, giving a brown flour high in gluten. Wholemeal flour or strong brown flour blended with plain flour provides an excellent alternative. For naan bread, use plain white flour or strong white flour.

Gram flour is made by milling lentils. It has a very distinctive flavour and texture and will give dishes in which it is used a yellowish colour. It is essential for making bhajis and pakoras. You can, in fact, make your own by grinding dried lentils in a coffee mill, but it is readily available in specialist and health-food shops.

If you extend your Balti repertoire you may find recipes that call for maize flour, rice flour or millet flour, but for the recipes in this book, those mentioned above will suffice.

PULSES AND LEGUMES

This group of ingredients forms a vital part of Balti cookery, and it will be helpful if you are familiar with the different types available.

Red split lentils are an orange-red colour and widely available in supermarkets. When cooked, they turn a pale mustard yellow and have a pleasant, mild and slightly nutty flavour.

Whole green lentils are round, flat and unsplit. They are a greenish brown colour, readily available, and cook quite quickly.

Yellow split peas are the equivalent in this country of "chana dal". They have small grains with a slightly sweet flavour. They are readily available and can be substituted for chana dal, which can only be found in specialist shops.

Black eyed beans are a pale beige colour, with a dark dot, hence their name. You should be able to find them in supermarkets, either dried or canned.

Red kidney beans justify their name by being dark red and kidney shaped. They have a good firm and nutty texture and are easily obtained both dried and canned.

Cooking times and methods are crucial for pulses and legumes, several of which also require soaking before cooking. You will find details of times and methods on pages 147-148.

If you have always considered lentils to be bland and unappetising, do give them another chance in Balti cookery. They have a special affinity for spicy flavours, make interesting dishes on their own, and provide texture and body to meat recipes.

CORIANDER

I have given a special section to coriander, the fresh green herb, because it is such a special part of Balti dishes. Although it is usually stirred in right at the end of the cooking time, or sometimes sprinkled on the top prior to serving, its wonderful flavour and aroma can transform almost any dish into an authentic masterpiece. The attractive shape and lush green colour of its leaves make it an excellent garnish - it could be considered the Indian version of parsley but with much more flavour! Usually just the leaves are used and the stalks are discarded, although they may be used to flavour a stock. The leaves may be finely or roughly chopped, depending on the appearance you wish to achieve.

Possibly the only disadvantage of coriander is that it is not always easy to find. Some supermarkets sell stalks of it and others have introduced little plants growing in pots. Sometimes these plants are too small to supply you with more than about a tablespoon of the herb. If you do find bunches of coriander for sale, keep it fresh by putting the stalks in a jug of cold water, as if you were putting flowers in a vase. It will keep fresh for several days and you can use it as required.

One way of ensuring that you always have a ready and cheap supply of coriander is to grow you own. The seeds germinate easily and you can soon have a tub full of attractive little plants. Keep them by your back door and they will release their wonderful fragrance every time you brush past them. As coriander is not frost hardy, bring a few of the more robust-looking plants indoors as the weather gets cooler and keep them on your kitchen windowsill. You could also harvest your crop, chop it and freeze it in small amounts (ice-cube trays are ideal) ready to add to your dishes. Do try making the delicious coriander chutney on page 178 - it adds zest to any meal.

YOGHURT

You will find that yoghurt appears in several Balti dishes - recognisably in raita and lassi, as a way of adding a creamy texture to sauces, and as a binding agent for naan bread. Most recipes will specify natural yoghurt, but if you look for this in your supermarket's dairy cabinet, you will be met by a bewildering choice. Yoghurt can be made from cow's, ewe's or goat's milk. It may be of normal consistency, set or thickened. It may contain active ingredients, in which case it is often called Bio yoghurt. It may be organic. It may be low fat, made with skimmed milk, or full fat, made with whole milk. You will also see Greek yoghurt and French set yoghurt.

Most Indian restaurants make their own yoghurt and generally use full cream milk. You can easily do the same (see page 62). In the recipes in this book, I have rarely specified a particular kind of yoghurt except where I have suggested that you use Greek yoghurt. This has a lovely, thick, rich, creamy texture and is particularly good dolloped on to the top of a dish just before serving.

Another use for yoghurt is in marinades, as in tandoori marinade (see page 59). It has a tenderising effect on meat and it mellows the flavours of spices in the marinade.

GARLIC

Nearly all the savoury recipes in this book include crushed garlic, usually sautéed with chopped onion at the beginning of a recipe. Garlic, of course, has a pungent flavour, but cooked garlic takes on a much more mellow note and adds a depth of flavour to any sauce. For this reason, the garlic should be fried for at least 5 minutes.

Garlic is usually added crushed, which brings out its full flavour. In fact, if you cook whole garlic cloves in a dish, they lose all their pungency. Chopped garlic has a mild flavour but crushing the clove allows all the aromatics to be released. I have seen chefs crushing a clove of garlic by smashing it with their fist, but pressing it with the flat of a broad-bladed knife is equally successful and people will be more inclined to shake hands with you afterwards.

When buying garlic, look for plump cloves with a papery outer skin and a pronounced garlic smell. The cloves should pull apart easily. Discard the outer skin and inner core. Chop the root end and top off the clove and peel off the final layer of skin. When a recipe calls for a clove, it means one of these individual segments, not the whole bulb. Of course, the individual cloves can vary in size - use your judgement as to how much is required.

Garlic is easy to grow yourself, too. Simply plant individual cloves and wait. They will put up green shoots, not unlike spring onions, and a bulb will develop under the soil. When harvested, allow the outer skin to dry before storing.

USING THESE
RECIPES

I f you have read the introductory sections of this book, you will now know what Balti is and what Balti cookery involves. You will be aware of what ingredients are used and how to handle them. Now we come to the most interesting part - cooking Balti recipes!

When you set out to cook a Balti dish, or indeed any dish, it is always a good idea to read through the recipe first, to make sure that you have all the necessary ingredients and equipment, including that needed for any pre-prepared ingredients listed in the recipe.

You will find that the first few recipes in each section are for fairly basic dishes. They are quite straightforward to make and ideal if you are rushing to prepare a midweek meal. I have also included some recipes that do not require any pre-preparation - all the spices you need are included in the recipe. These are great if you are in a hurry and have no pre-prepared mixes to hand. If you are new to Balti cookery, you may like to start with these to make sure you enjoy the experience. In the extremely unlikely event that you don't, you will not then have a cupboard full of redundant spices and a freezer full of Balti sauce.

Once you are sure that Balti is for you, don't hesitate to pre-prepare sauces and mixes and stock up the freezer with par-cooked meat and cooked lentils and pulses. This will make cooking a Balti dish whenever you feel like it simplicity itself.

All the recipes in this book have both metric and imperial measures, but as these are rounded up or down to make easy-to-measure amounts, it is very important that you stick to either metric or imperial measures in one recipe and don't alternate between the two. Having said that, do remember too that when it comes to different spices and flavourings, any measurement is only a guide. Ingredients can vary quite widely in their strength and you will also have your own likes and dislikes. Add more chilli if you enjoy hot dishes; include more fresh coriander if you like its sharply pungent flavour.

Likewise, oven temperatures in the recipes are given in degrees Centigrade, Fahrenheit and Gas Marks. You will know the idiosyncrasies of your own oven, so adapt these if necessary.

I can't repeat too many times that one of the great joys of Balti cookery is the flexibility it allows you. Make a few of the dishes by following the recipes closely, then, when you are familiar with the basics of Balti, throw caution to the winds and experiment. Who knows if bacon and banana Balti isn't a great dish waiting to be invented?

CONVERSION TABLES

Remember...

Use metric or imperial measures, not both.

Spoon measures are level, unless otherwise specified.

The recipes in this book are based on size 3 eggs, but size 2 or 4 will be fine.

Where a recipe calls for a pinch of a particular spice, it is literally the amount you can pick up between your thumb and forefinger.

WEIGHTS

$\frac{1}{2}$oz	10g	7oz	200g
1oz	25g	8oz	225g
1$\frac{1}{2}$oz	40g	9oz	250g
2oz	50g	10oz	275g
2$\frac{1}{2}$oz	60g	11oz	300g
3oz	75g	12oz	350g
3$\frac{1}{2}$oz	90g	14oz	400g
4oz	110g	1lb	450g
4$\frac{1}{2}$oz	125g	1$\frac{1}{2}$lb	700g
5oz	150g	2lb	900g
6oz	175g	3lb	1.5kg (1500g)

MEASUREMENTS

1/8 inch	3mm		1 1/2 inches	4cm
1/4 inch	5mm		2 inches	5cm
1/2 inch	1cm		3 inches	7.5cm
3/4 inch	2cm		4 inches	10cm
1 inch	2.5cm		12 inches	30cm
1 1/4 inches	3cm			

LIQUID MEASURES

5 fl oz	1/4pt	150ml	15 fl oz	3/4pt	425ml
7.5 fl oz	-	215ml	20 fl oz	1pt	570ml
10 fl oz	1/2pt	275ml	35 fl oz	1 3/4pt	1 litre

SPOON MEASURES

1/2 tspn	2.5ml		2tbspn	30ml
1tspn	5ml		3tbspn	45ml
1 1/2tspn	7.5ml		4tbspn	60ml
2tspn	10ml		5tbspn	75ml
1tbspn	15ml			

OVEN TEMPERATURES

Gas Mark 1	275°F	140°C	Gas Mark 5	375°F	190°C
Gas Mark 2	300°F	150°C	Gas Mark 6	400°F	200°C
Gas Mark 3	325°F	170°C	Gas Mark 7	425°F	220°C
Gas Mark 4	350°F	180°C	Gas Mark 8	450°F	230°C

ABBREVIATIONS

cm	centimetre		mm	millimetre
fl oz	fluid ounce		oz	ounce
g	gram		pt	pint
kg	kilogram		tbspn	tablespoon
ml	millilitre		tspn	teaspoon

BALTI BASICS

RECIPES

1 GHEE

Clarified butter is used in many of the recipes in this book. Why not make your own?

2 BALTI SPICE MIX

A basic mix of the spices that appear in many of the recipes

3 BALTI GARAM MASALA

One recipe incorporating grinding whole spices and a quicker version

using commercially ground spices

4 BALTI SAUCE

The basis of many recipes

5 QUICK BALTI SAUCE

A version of this Balti basic for emergencies

6 TANDOORI MARINADE

A spicy marinade for tandoori and tikka meat and poultry with recipes for

basic dishes

7 YOGHURT

A whole-milk recipe as made in Balti houses

A s you leaf through the recipes in this book, you will see that time and again they call for a spoonful of Balti sauce, a pinch of garam masala or some chicken tikka. The recipes for these will all be found in this section - they are, if you like, your Balti building blocks.

The actual final stir-frying of a Balti is a very quick process, but it needs the foundations to be in place. Your meal preparation will be much quicker if you can run to the freezer and pull out a pot of Balti sauce, or reach into the cupboard for a jar of your secret spice mix.

I have also included a recipe for yoghurt. Of course, this is designed for use in the recipes in this book, but try some into which jam, honey or some sweetened stewed fruit has been stirred - you may never buy ready made yoghurt again!

Remember, the recipes in this section are a guide. Just as no two recipes for steak and kidney pudding are the same, so spice mixes are a matter of personal taste. Try these recipes without changes first - they will give you a starting point from which to shape your own, individual recipes. Then your Balti dishes will be the talk of your friends and impossible to copy - your spice mix is your secret.

♣ GHEE ♣

Ghee is clarified butter. You will find that it appears in many of the recipes in this book and that usually vegetable oil is offered as an alternative. However, if you are planning to cook several Balti recipes, then the time spent making ghee is worthwhile. Because the milk solids have been removed, ghee can be heated to a high temperature without burning and doesn't need to be refrigerated, although a cool storage place is preferable. It is probably in the bread recipes that the flavour of ghee is most distinct, and as breads are such an important part of Balti cuisine, ghee is worth trying at least once.

MAKES: 350G (12OZ)

PREPARATION TIME: ABOUT 1 HOUR

450g (1lb) unsalted butter

1 Place the whole piece of butter in a non-stick saucepan or one with a heavy base. Melt the butter over a very low heat.

2 When the butter is totally melted, raise the heat slightly. Leave the butter to "cook" for about an hour, without stirring. Don't be tempted to try to speed up the process by turning up the heat - the mixture will burn, which will taint the fat and render it unusable. During cooking, the impurities in the butter will either sink to the bottom of the pan or float on top of the liquid fat. Using a slotted spoon, carefully skim off the floating residue, but don't touch that at the bottom.

3 Remove the pan from the heat and allow it to cool. Strain into a container (a coffee filter-paper is useful for this) and discard the residue.

❧ BALTI SPICE MIX ❧

This is simply a collection of the spices that appear in many Baltis. To save time, make up a batch of this mix and store it in a screw-top jar. Then you have it to hand whenever you want to make a Balti. Making up a batch also means that quantities can be more accurate, as you are dealing with teaspoons rather than pinches.

MAKES: 30ML (2TBSPN OR 6TSPN)

PREPARATION TIME: SECONDS!

10ml (2tspn) paprika

2.5ml ($^{1}/_{2}$tspn) chilli powder

5ml (1tspn) salt

7.5ml (1$^{1}/_{2}$tspn) ground coriander

5ml (1tspn) ground cumin

Simply mix everything together thoroughly and store in a screw-top jar.

Cook's tip

Chilli powders vary enormously. Here you need just a hint of warmth in the spice mix. If you like your food very spicy, you can add more chilli powder in the final recipe - which may also include chopped green chillies.

♣ BALTI GARAM MASALA ♣

This literally means a hot (garam) mixture of spices (masala). In Indian dishes it is often used as a seasoning, in much the same way that salt and pepper are added in European cooking, and it is usually incorporated towards the end of the cooking time. As with all classic recipes, there are hundreds of variations on garam masala and no single correct version. You will probably find yourself adapting these basic recipes to suit your own taste - good! Aren't the best recipe books the ones that are full of scribbles and adaptations where the recipes have been "adjusted"? For example, one of the recipes below includes star anise. This may be authentic, but if you don't like aniseed, out it goes!

I have included two recipes here. One uses whole spices and is for those who enjoy grinding and roasting their own spices. The other is a blend of ready ground spices, for when time is short. Both give perfectly acceptable results.

GARAM MASALA 1

MAKES: 75ML (5TBSPN OR 15TSPN)

PREPARATION TIME: 5 MINUTES + GRINDING TIME

15ml (1tbspn) cumin seeds

15ml (1tbspn) cardamom pods

5ml (1tspn) cloves

15ml (1tbspn) black peppercorns

5cm (2 inch) stick of cinnamon, broken in half

2 star anise

4 bay leaves

5ml (1tspn) dried mint leaves

1 Gently roast all the spices, taking care not to burn them. Cool.

2 Grind all the spices to a fine powder and store in an air-tight screw-top jar.

GARAM MASALA 2

MAKES: 50ML (10TSPN)

PREPARATION TIME: 5 MINUTES

15ml (1tbspn) ground coriander

2.5ml ($^1/_2$tspn) ground bay

15ml (1tbspn) ground cardamom

10ml (2tspn) ground cumin

2.5ml ($^1/_2$tspn) ground black pepper

2.5ml ($^1/_2$tspn) ground cinnamon

2.5ml ($^1/_2$tspn) ground cloves

Carefully measure out the spices and mix them together thoroughly. Then store in an air-tight screw-top jar.

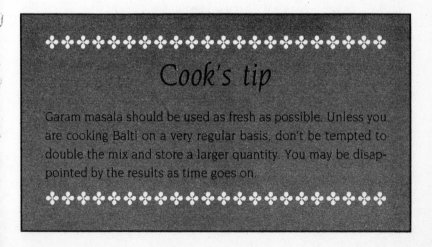

Cook's tip

Garam masala should be used as fresh as possible. Unless you are cooking Balti on a very regular basis, don't be tempted to double the mix and store a larger quantity. You may be disappointed by the results as time goes on.

✤ BALTI SAUCE ✤

As with garam masala, there are probably as many recipes for Balti sauce as there are people cooking Baltis. As it is the basis for many recipes, you need to be sure that the one you use is to your liking. Make this basic recipe first, then adjust it to suit your preferences - more spicy, less tomato, no garlic and so on.

MAKES: 1 LITRE (1³/₄ PINTS)

PREPARATION TIME: ABOUT 50-60 MINUTES

45ml (3tbspn) vegetable oil

2.5cm (1 inch) cube fresh ginger, grated

6 onions, peeled and chopped

2 cloves garlic, peeled and finely chopped

5ml (1tspn) ground cumin

10ml (2tspn) ground coriander

2.5ml (¹/₂tspn) chilli powder

2.5ml (¹/₂tspn) turmeric powder

5ml (1tspn) garam masala

5 cardamom pods, lightly crushed

2 bay leaves

5ml (1tspn) dried fenugreek leaves

5 tomatoes, peeled and chopped

10ml (2tspn) tomato purée

1 Heat the oil in a large pan over a medium heat. Add the onions, garlic and ginger and cook, stirring, until the onion is cooked and just beginning to turn brown at the edges.

2 Add all the spices and cook gently for a few minutes. Now add the tomatoes and tomato purée. Mix well and add 275ml ($^1/_2$pt) of water. Bring to the boil and simmer for 30-40 minutes.

3 Remove the bay leaf and cardamom pods (count them in and count them out!) and cool the sauce.

4 Place the sauce in a liquidiser or food processor and purée until smooth. Store, covered, in the refrigerator for up to a week, or freeze in small batches and defrost as required.

❖❖❖❖❖❖❖❖❖❖❖❖❖❖❖❖❖❖❖❖❖❖❖❖❖❖❖❖

Cook's tip

If you don't own a food processor or liquidiser, you can still make this sauce by pushing the finished mix through a sieve. In this case, do try to chop the onions and tomatoes as finely as possible - time spent at the beginning will be time saved at the end.

❖❖❖❖❖❖❖❖❖❖❖❖❖❖❖❖❖❖❖❖❖❖❖❖❖❖❖❖

♣ QUICK BALTI SAUCE ♣

This recipe will not have the depth of flavour of the previous one, but there may be occasions when you have no Balti sauce to hand for use in a recipe and no time to make the full version. You may find the quick sauce a little runnier but to compensate you can adjust the amount of water that you add to the recipe in which you are using this. If you need an even quicker version, replace all the spices with 15ml (1tbspn) of Balti spice mix (see page 53) if you have some prepared.

MAKES: ABOUT 570ML (1PT)

PREPARATION TIME: 30 MINUTES

45ml (3tbspn) ghee or vegetable oil

2 onions, finely chopped

1 clove garlic, crushed

5ml (1tspn) paprika

5ml (1tspn) ground coriander

2.5ml ($^1/_2$tspn) ground cumin

Generous pinch of each of salt, chilli powder and ground ginger

400g (14oz) can chopped tomatoes in natural juice

1 Heat the ghee or oil in a Balti pan, wok or saucepan over a medium to high heat. Add the onions and garlic and sizzle for about 10 minutes, stirring from time to time, until soft and golden brown.

2 Add the spices and salt and cook, stirring, for 2 minutes.

3 Add the tomatoes, with their juice, and bring to the boil. Simmer for 15 minutes, stirring occasionally.

4 Liquidise the sauce in a food processor or liquidiser, or push through a sieve.

♣ TANDOORI MARINADE ♣

In several recipes in this book, you will need tandoori or tikka meat, poultry or fish. The basic difference between tandoori and tikka is that tandoori tends to be larger, bone-in pieces, while tikka is smaller, boneless cuts.

MAKES: 450G (1 LB)

PREPARATION TIME: 15 MINUTES

30ml (2tbspn) vegetable oil

30g (1oz) fresh root ginger, grated

30ml (2tbspn) tomato purée

2 large cloves garlic, peeled and crushed

15ml (1tbspn) lemon juice

1 large green chilli, finely chopped

10g ($^1/_2$oz) salt

5ml (1tspn) ground cumin

5ml (1tspn) ground coriander

5ml (1tspn) chilli powder

25g (1oz) fresh coriander, chopped

15ml (1tbspn) red food colour (optional)

15ml (1tbspn) orange food colour (optiona)

275ml ($^1/_2$pt) natural whole-milk yoghurt

Blend the vegetable oil, ginger, tomato purée, garlic, lemon juice and green chilli. Add the salt and spices and mix well. Stir in the fresh coriander and the food colour, if using. Blend in the yoghurt until very thoroughly mixed. Use in the following recipes or store in a covered container in the refrigerator for up to five days.

✤ TANDOORI/TIKKA CHICKEN ✤

For this recipe, use part-boned breast portions, drumsticks or thighs. Cooking the meat on the bone gives added succulence and flavour, and it can easily be taken off the bone once cooled and cooked. Making this recipe will take your cooker to temperatures it may never have reached before - close any doors between your cooker and your smoke detector! Start this dish the day before you need it.

MAKES: 1KG (2.2LB) COOKED MEAT

PREPARATION TIME: ABOUT 24 HOURS (MOSTLY MARINATING)

1.5kg (3lb) chicken breast portions, drumsticks or thighs, or a mixture

450g (1lb) tandoori marinade

1 Cut deep slits, about three per portion, in the chicken and place it in a bowl. Add the tandoori marinade and tumble the meat around in it, using your hands, until the pieces are evenly coated. Cover the bowl with cling film and leave to chill overnight.

2 Preheat your oven to its highest setting. Arrange the chicken in a single layer on a baking tray, smoothing out the marinade to give a thin, even coating.

3 Place the tray in the oven and cook for about 25 minutes. Test that the chicken is cooked by piercing with a sharp knife - the juices should be clear and the outside should be dry and slightly charred around the edges.

4 Allow the chicken to cool on the tray, before removing from the bone if tikka meat is required. The cooked meat can be successfully frozen.

♣ TANDOORI LAMB ♣

Make as for tandoori chicken but use boneless meat, cut into 4cm ($1^{1}/_{2}$ inch) cubes. There is no need to cut slits in the meat as the pieces are smaller. Marinate and cook in the same way, allowing about 30-35 minutes. You may like the meat to remain a little pink in the centre after cooking.

♣ TANDOORI FISH ♣

Use 2.5cm (1 inch) chunks of firm white fish, such as cod or haddock. Again, there is no need to cut slits in the fish. Marinate and cook the fish as in the chicken recipe, allowing about 15 minutes cooking time. The fish should flake apart but still retain some moistness.

Large prawns with the shell removed can be treated in exactly the same way. Use them in recipes or serve as a delicious starter.

♣ YOGHURT ♣

Several recipes in this book include yoghurt. Of course, commercially produced varieties are fine, but if you have the time to make your own, you can be sure that the resulting dishes will be on a par with some of the top Balti restaurants.

MAKES: 570ML (1PT)

PREPARATION TIME: 8 HOURS

570ml (1pt) full cream milk
15ml (1tbspn) natural yoghurt

1 Place the milk in a heavy-based saucepan and bring to the boil. As soon as the milk starts to rise in the pan, take it off the heat and leave to cool to between 38 and 43°C (100 and 110°F). This should just feel warm to the touch.

2 Whisk the yoghurt in a small bowl and slowly beat in the warm milk, including the skin that will have formed.

3 Cover the bowl with cling film and leave in a warm place at around 30-38°C (85-100°F) for 8 hours, until the yoghurt has set. The airing cupboard or warming drawer of the oven are often the best places for this.

4 Chill the yoghurt and store it in the refrigerator for up to five days.

POULTRY AND
GAME

RECIPES

1 BASIC CHICKEN BALTI

An ideal introduction to Balti cooking

2 CHICKEN AND CHICK PEA BALTI

A very quick and easy dish

3 CHICKEN AND MUSHROOM BALTI

Baby mushrooms and chicken combine wonderfully in this dish

4 FRUITY CHICKEN BALTI

A delicious and versatile combination

5 SHREDDED CHICKEN BALTI

The chicken in this recipe is marinated for an hour before cooking

6 COCONUT CHICKEN BALTI

Coconut milk adds a wonderful flavour and texture to this dish

7 BALTI TIKKA MASALA

The Balti version of a restaurant favourite

8 CHICKEN AND PRAWN BALTI

A very popular fish and chicken combination

9 CHICKEN BALTI WITH FRIED VEGETABLES

The vegetables are slightly charred to give a delicious flavour in this recipe

10 DUCK BALTI

Orange zest and juice add to the flavours in this special dish

11 CHICKEN BALTI WITH CREAM AND YOGHURT SAUCE

A rich and creamy treat for a special occasion

12 BALTI DRUMSTICKS

Sweetcorn makes this a colourful dish

13 CHICKEN AND EGG BALTI

Chicken and egg are served together in a creamy Balti sauce

14 BALTI ROGAN JOSH

Another restaurant favourite in Balti style

15 QUAIL BALTI

An exotic Balti dish using halved quails

16 BALTI STIR FRY

A quick-to-prepare dish that need never be the same twice!

Poultry and game particularly lend themselves to the quick, stir-fry method of Balti cooking and there is such a huge variety to choose from that the following recipes are really just a guide - you could use any of the birds mentioned in this introduction, instead of the meat specified.

In most Balti recipes poultry is used skinless and off the bone. This makes the meat easier to cook, serve and eat. It is usually possible to buy prepared poultry, particularly chicken and turkey, from supermarkets, and certainly a good butcher would cut up a bird for you. However, it is surprisingly easy to joint a whole bird, and de-bone the breast and thighs yourself. Instructions for this are given below. The bones and leftovers can be used to make chicken stock. If your first efforts leave rather a lot of meat on the bone, then you will simply have a richer stock!

Research has shown that when ordering curries in restaurants, nearly 60% of customers choose a poultry-based main course. This reflects the growing popularity of poultry - chicken now outranks beef as the most popular meat. There are probably four reasons for this. Firstly, chicken is readily available, in a wide range of sizes and portions. Secondly, it is a very economical choice of meat. Thirdly, it is a healthy option, in particular lower in saturated fats than red meats. Finally, as the recipes that follow will show, it is extremely versatile. Chicken does not have an overpowering flavour of its own and is therefore receptive to many ingredients and flavourings.

In the next section you will find a guide to poultry and game, with ideas on basic preparation, followed by a number of specific recipes. There are no par-cooking details because in most dishes the meat is used diced and cooks very quickly. But if you have leftover cooked poultry or game, then do by all means use it, adjusting the cooking times as necessary.

CHICKEN

Probably the first bird to become domesticated and said to have originated in India, this is the most popular of all poultry.

Arguments will always occur about free-range versus battery hens. People are rightly concerned both about the humane issue and the question of flavour. If you buy your poultry from a leading supermarket or reputable butcher, you can be sure that the birds have been reared and killed under strict guidelines laid down by both the retailer and the Government. Certainly one might expect free-range birds to have more flavour, but when combined with the many spices and seasonings used in Balti recipes, this is not of major importance.

Most oven-ready chickens sold are in the weight range of 1-2.7kg (2.2-6lb). Choose plump birds, with no visible bruising, that are a healthy pink colour. The exception to this is corn-fed birds, which will have a yellowish tinge to the skin. Check the label carefully to ensure that this is due to the corn and not the addition of artificial colourings to the bird's food.

To joint a chicken, first remove the wings. Pull them away from the body and cut through the joint, trimming carefully so you do not cut away too much of the breast meat. Next remove the legs, again pulling them away from the carcass and cutting through the joint. You should be able to feel where the joint is - rest the knife on this point and cut sharply through. Divide the drumstick and thigh at the chicken's equivalent of a knee. You will need a heavy, sharp knife that is longer than the chicken to cut away the backbone. Remember, that's the side that's underneath when the curved breast is pointing upwards! Place the carcass, backbone down, on a chopping board. Insert the knife into the cavity of the chicken at one end so the point comes out the other end. Press down hard on the handle and the top of the tip of the blade that is poking out and cut one side of the backbone. Repeat on the other side. If you want the breast on the bone, simply cut down the middle where the breasts join. For boneless meat, remove the skin and position on a board with the neck-end facing you. Feel between the two breasts and you will discover a strip of cartilage and bone. Run a sharp, thin knife either side of this and over the wishbone. Carefully start pulling the fillet away, scraping the knife against the bone to ensure the small, anatomical fillet also comes away. Trim off the carcass at the base. To de-bone the thighs, lay them on a board, skin side down, and run a small, sharp knife either side of the bone, so that it is loosened. Now slide the knife under the bone, and pull it away. One end will be held on by a piece of cartilage. Trim this away. Remember, the meat will probably be diced in your recipe, so do not worry if it does not look perfect at this stage.

The meat on a drumstick is full of sinews and not really worth de-boning. Breast and thigh meat are the best cuts for Balti dishes and in most cases should be diced to about 2.5cm (1 inch) cubes.

TURKEY

It is only in recent years that turkey has stopped being a once-a-year treat and has become an economical meat available all year round. Turkeys tend to be large. Anything between 2.7 and 5kg (6 and 10lb) is a typical oven-ready weight, but if you buy a fresh one there is no reason why you cannot cut off the meat, dice it and freeze it in packs suitable for your family size. Alternatively, turkey breast joints, fillets and thighs are readily available and can be de-boned as for chicken. A further option is turkey mince. A healthier alternative to minced red meat, it can replace the mince used in the recipes in the Meat section of this book. Specialised breeds of turkey, such as Bronze and Norfolk Black are now available and undoubtedly have a superior flavour, but they tend to be more expensive and are usually only available around Christmas and Easter. They are not essential for Balti cookery.

DUCK

The Chinese first domesticated the duck thousands of years ago and anyone who has eaten crispy Peking duck will agree that they know a thing or two about cooking them. The most important thing when cooking duck is to get rid of the excess fat. For the Balti style of cooking, this really means using only the breast and removing all skin and the layer of fat beneath it. On the commonly available Lincolnshire duck, this amounts to a disappointingly large proportion of the breast fillet. Barbary duck breasts, available in most large supermarkets and usually imported from France, have a much thinner fat layer. However, for Balti cookery this must be removed, together with the skin. You will find it quite loose around the edges, but you will have to carefully pare it away from the flesh, using a sharp knife, in the centre of the fillet. The resultant lean meat will be quite expensive - three fillets will serve four people - but will make a delicious treat for a special occasion.

GOOSE

Goose provides a "halfway house" between poultry and game. It has a distinctly "gamey" flavoured flesh that can become quite tough on larger birds. Choose an oven-ready goose weighing 2.7-3.5kg (6-8lb). This may sound large, but the meat-to-bone ratio on a goose is not good and there is also a lot of fat. Goose is another meat best saved for special occasions.

GAME BIRDS

Game birds may seem rather luxurious for inclusion in a Balti cookbook, but remember that the Balti people were nomadic. This meant that they foraged for food and to these hunters game birds were of one of the most common sources of protein.

In Britain fresh game is seasonal, on sale in autumn and winter, but some varieties are reared in captivity, and are more readily available.

PHEASANT

This is stocked in most supermarkets in season, but can quite often be found in freezer cabinets at other times of the year. If you are buying from a butcher and want to justify spending more on ready dressed birds, remember that by buying a bird with the feathers removed you can check that it has not been badly shot - birds shot in the wing or head are best, as the prime meat of the breast is left intact. The female birds tend to be younger and more tender, but often buying a brace - a male and a female - is a more economical option. A pheasant should serve three people.

GROUSE

This bird, which becomes fair game on the "Glorious 12th" of August, is much prized for the flavour of its meat. Most of us are not lucky enough to be served grouse very often, and you may perhaps prefer to serve this particular game bird more traditionally.

GUINEA FOWL

This is now a farmed game bird, readily available from both France and this country. It looks not unlike a thin, small chicken, although the flesh has a yellowish tinge and the meat has a moderately gamey flavour, not unlike a mild pheasant. An average-sized bird will comfortably feed four.

PARTRIDGE

A relative of the pheasant, but smaller, a partridge will provide a generous portion of meat for one person.

QUAIL

Also now being farmed, quail are tiny birds - two for a single portion would not be excessive. They are normally cooked whole, although a major supermarket sells them partially de-boned and stuffed.

Other game birds, including pigeon and snipe, can, of course, be used in the recipes in place of the poultry or game suggested.

One final point when cooking poultry is that it must be thoroughly cooked. Many people enjoy their lamb pink and their steaks rare, but poultry must always be tested to check that the meat is fully cooked through before serving. A quick test is to push a skewer or fork into the centre of the meat. The meat should come away from the bone, if any, very easily and the juices should run clear, not at all pink. If you are serving those who should take special care not to eat undercooked poultry ~ the elderly, the very young or pregnant women ~ you may wish to use a meat thermometer. The meat should have reached 75°C (105°F) to be safe. When you are reheating refrigerated or defrosted poultry Balti dishes, you should take the same care that they are heated through thoroughly.

♣ BASIC CHICKEN BALTI ♣

At the beginning of each chapter of Balti recipes you will find a "basic" dish. If you are new to Balti cookery, it may be helpful to make this recipe exactly as suggested. This will then provide you with a kind of "standard" from which to make your own variations and adaptations.

SERVES: 4

PREPARATION TIME: 30 MINUTES

700g (1½lb) skinless, boneless chicken, cut into 2.5cm (1 inch) cubes

45ml (3tbspn) ghee or vegetable oil

4 cloves garlic, crushed

2 large onions, finely chopped

45ml (3tbspn) Balti garam masala (see page 54)

200ml (7 fl oz) water

15ml (1tbspn) coriander leaves, finely chopped

Salt and pepper

1 Heat two-thirds of the ghee or oil in a Balti pan, wok or large frying pan. Add the onion and garlic and cook over a medium heat for about 10 minutes until softened.

2 Meanwhile mix two-thirds of the garam masala with the remaining spoonful of oil and enough of the water to make a stiff paste. Add this to the onions with the chicken. Mix well and stir fry for 5 minutes.

3 Add the rest of the water, reduce to a simmer and cook for about 10 minutes. Test a piece of chicken by cutting it in half - it should be white all the way through with no trace of pinkness.

4. Add the coriander and remaining garam masala and cook for a further 2-3 minutes. Season to taste. Serve.

♣ CHICKEN AND CHICK PEA BALTI ♣

This is another good beginner's Balti that is very quick to prepare - the only pre-preparation needed is to make the garam masala. This recipe features chick peas, which crop up quite often in Balti recipes. I have used canned peas but if you wish to cook your own, see page 147.

SERVES: 4

PREPARATION TIME: 35 MINUTES

450g (1lb) chicken breast, diced into 2.5cm (1 inch) cubes

30ml (2tbspn) ghee or vegetable oil

2 cloves garlic, crushed

1 large onion, finely chopped

5ml (1tspn) chilli powder

10ml (2tspn) ground coriander

400g (14oz) can chick peas, drained

400g (14oz) can chopped tomatoes

15ml (1tbspn) Balti garam masala (see page 54)

15ml (1tbspn) fresh coriander, roughly chopped

1 Heat the ghee or oil in a Balti pan, wok or large frying pan. Add the onion and garlic and cook over a medium heat for about 10 minutes, until starting to brown.

2 Add the chicken and stir fry for 5 minutes. Add the chilli powder and ground coriander and mix well.

3 Add the chick peas and tomatoes, reduce the heat and simmer for 15 minutes.

4 Stir in the garam masala and cook for a further 2 minutes. Add the chopped coriander and serve.

♣ CHICKEN AND MUSHROOM BALTI ♣

In this recipe you can use light or dark chicken meat or a combination of both. Little baby button mushrooms look particularly attractive in this dish - they are more fiddly to slice but worth it!

SERVES: 4

PREPARATION TIME: 40 MINUTES

700g (1½lb) chicken, cut into 2.5cm (1 inch) cubes

30ml (2tbspn) ghee or vegetable oil

2 large onions, chopped

4 cloves garlic, crushed

2 fresh green chillies, finely chopped

2.5cm (1 inch) cube fresh root ginger, grated

10ml (2tspn) Balti spice mix (see page 53)

15ml (1tspn) dried fenugreek leaves

150ml (¼pt) Balti sauce (see page 56)

110g (4oz) Button mushrooms, sliced

15ml (1tbspn) Balti garam masala (see page 54)

15ml (1tbspn) fresh coriander, chopped

Salt and pepper

1 Heat the ghee or oil in a Balti pan, wok or large frying pan. Add the onions and garlic and stir fry over a medium heat for 5 minutes. Add the green chillies and ginger and cook for a further 5 minutes.

2 Stir in the chicken and spice mix and cook, stirring, for 10 minutes.

3 Add the fenugreek leaves and Balti sauce, mix and reduce the heat. Simmer for 15 minutes.

4 Add the mushrooms and garam masala and cook for a further 5 minutes. Stir in the coriander, season if required. Serve.

♣ FRUITY CHICKEN BALTI ♣

Fruit and chicken have always been served together - apples in Chicken Normande, bananas in Chicken Maryland, grapes in Chicken Veronique. Apricots, lemons and prunes are other classic accompaniments. Here the choice of fruit is really up to you. Pineapple has been used in the recipe below, but mango or a mixture of the two would also work well.

SERVES: 4

PREPARATION TIME: 40 MINUTES

700g (1½lb) boneless chicken, diced to about the same size as the pineapple cubes

30ml (2tbspn) ghee or vegetable oil

2 large onions, sliced

2 large cloves garlic, crushed

2.5cm (1 inch) cube fresh ginger, grated

15ml (1tbspn) Balti spice mix (see page 53)

A generous pinch of each of ground cloves, ground cinnamon, ground bay leaves and ground black pepper

15ml (1tbspn) lemon juice

About 175g (6oz) pineapple chunks canned in natural juice, drained

15ml (1tbspn) juice from can of pineapple

15ml (1tbspn) fresh coriander, chopped

1 Heat the ghee or oil in a Balti pan, wok or large frying pan. Add the onions and garlic and cook over a medium heat for 5 minutes. Add the ginger and all the spices and cook, stirring, for a further 5 minutes.

2 Add the chicken plus 60ml (4tbspn) water, and stir fry for 15-20 minutes, until just tender.

3 Add the lemon juice, pineapple chunks and pineapple juice. Simmer for 5 minutes, adding extra water if necessary.

4 Add the coriander and simmer for a further 2 minutes. Serve.

Cook's tip

You can, of course, use fresh pineapple in this dish. Check that it is ripe before buying by gently tugging at one of the leaves at the top. It should come away easily. To prepare the pineapple, slice off the stalk and leaf ends, stand the fruit on end, then shave slices down the sides to remove the skin. You will need a sharp knife and strong downward strokes, following the shape of the pineapple. When you have done this, there will still be brown pits in the flesh. You can remove these one by one with the point of a sharp knife, or you can cut down in spirals, removing a shallow v-shape round the pineapple. Then cut the pineapple into slices about 2cm (¾ inch) thick and cut these into cubes. If the pineapple is very ripe, the core can be eaten, but you should discard it if it is hard or woody.

♣ SHREDDED CHICKEN BALTI ♣

The flavour in this recipe comes from the marinated meat. Ideally you need a liquidiser or food processor to make the marinade paste, but a pestle and mortar and a bit of elbow grease works just as well. This produces a dry curry, ideal to serve with a saucy, vegetable Balti.

SERVES: 4

PREPARATION TIME: 25 MINUTES + 1 HOUR MARINATING TIME

450g (1lb) chicken breast fillet, shredded into thin strips

2 green chillies

3 cloves garlic, peeled

2.5cm (1 inch) cube fresh root ginger, grated

1 large onion, roughly chopped

15ml (1tbspn) vinegar or lemon juice

15ml (1tbspn) Balti spice mix

25ml (2tbspn) ghee or vegetable oil

1 green and 1 red pepper, cored, deseeded and thinly sliced

1 In a food processor or liquidiser whiz together the chillies, garlic, ginger, onion and vinegar or lemon juice.

2 Mix with the chicken and leave in a cool place to marinate for at least 1 hour. Mix in the Balti spice mix.

3 Heat the ghee or oil in a Balti pan, wok or large frying pan over a medium to high heat. Add the chicken and paste and stir fry for about 10-15 minutes.

4 Add the peppers and cook for a further 10 minutes, until the chicken is tender and cooked and the peppers have started to soften.

♣ COCONUT CHICKEN BALTI ♣

Coconut milk adds a wonderful flavour and texture to a sauce. This used to be rather difficult to find except in specialist shops, but now coconut milk powder is available in most supermarkets. Keep a packet handy in the cupboard to reconstitute when you need it.

SERVES: 4

PREPARATION TIME: 30 MINUTES

700g (1½lb) boneless chicken, cut into 2.5cm (1 inch) cubes

30ml (2tbspn) ghee or vegetable oil

10ml (2tspn) mustard seeds

2 fresh green chillies, finely chopped

10ml (2tspn) Balti spice mix (see page 53)

75g (3oz) coconut powder

Desiccated coconut

15ml (1tbspn) fresh coriander, roughly chopped

Lemon juice

1 Heat the ghee or oil in a Balti pan, wok or large frying pan, over a medium heat. Add the chicken and stir fry for about 5 minutes, until all the edges are sealed.

2 Add the mustard seeds, chillies and spice mix and stir well.

3 Mix the coconut powder with enough water to make a paste the consistency of tomato ketchup. Add two-thirds of this to the pan and simmer for 20 minutes. Meanwhile, add water to the remaining coconut paste to give it the consistency of milk. Add this during the cooking time to make quite a thin sauce.

4 Garnish with coconut and coriander, and serve with a little lemon juice squeezed over each portion.

♣ BALTI TIKKA MASALA ♣

Here is a great Indian restaurant favourite given a Balti twist. Pre-cooked tandoori chicken taken off the bone forms the basis of this recipe, or you could cheat and use some commercially prepared chicken tikka. Most supermarkets have their own brand.

SERVES: 4

PREPARATION TIME: 25 MINUTES

700g (1½lb) pre-cooked, de-boned tandoori chicken, cut into 3cm (11/4 inch)
cubes - thighs work well in this dish

45ml (3tbspn) ghee or vegetable oil

2 large onions, finely chopped

2.5cm (1 inch) cube fresh root ginger, grated

About 150ml (¼pt) Balti sauce (see page 56)

15ml (1tbspn) ground almonds

10ml (2tspn) coconut milk powder, mixed with water to a runny paste

15ml (1tbspn) tomato purée

15ml (1tbspn) dried fenugreek

150ml (¼pt) single cream

Flaked almonds

1 Heat the ghee or oil in a Balti pan, wok or large frying pan over a medium heat. Add the onions and stir fry until golden brown - about 10 minutes.

2 Add the ginger and chicken and mix well. Stir in most of the Balti sauce and add the almonds, coconut milk paste, tomato purée and fenugreek. Bring to a simmer and slowly add the cream.

3 Simmer gently for 12 minutes, adding a little more Balti sauce if the mix becomes dry. Serve, sprinkled with flaked almonds.

♣ CHICKEN AND PRAWN BALTI ♣

Combining meat and fish is quite common in Balti dishes and if you make this one you'll know why - it's delicious. For this dish exotic prawns are not necessary. Those sold as "cooking" prawns are fine.

SERVES: 4

PREPARATION TIME: 35 MINUTES

450g (1lb) chicken, cut into 2.5cm (1 inch) cubes

175g (6oz) peeled prawns (weighed after defrosting and draining, if frozen)

30ml (2tbspn) ghee or vegetable oil

2 large onions, chopped

2 cloves garlic, crushed

2 fresh green chillies, finely chopped

5ml (1tspn) Balti spice mix (see page 53)

5ml (1tspn) turmeric

1 small green pepper, deseeded and finely sliced

Pinch of Balti garam masala (see page 54)

15ml (1tbspn) fresh coriander, chopped

1 Heat the ghee or oil in a Balti pan, wok or large frying pan over a medium heat. Add the onions and garlic and cook until golden brown - about 10 minutes.

2 Add the chicken, chillies, spice mix and turmeric and stir fry for about 10 minutes.

3 Add the prawns, green pepper and about 100ml (4 fl oz) water. Simmer gently for 15 minutes until the chicken is cooked and the pepper is just tender.

4 Serve, sprinkled with garam masala and coriander.

♣ CHICKEN BALTI WITH FRIED ♣ VEGETABLES

I have chosen my own favourite vegetables for this dish, but of course you could use any kinds you wish - vegetables that are good when fried are best. By cooking the vegetables in hot oil you will start to char them, releasing delicious flavours.

SERVES: 4

PREPARATION TIME: 45 MINUTES

700g (1½lb) boneless chicken, diced

1 fresh green chilli, finely chopped

2 cloves garlic, crushed

120ml (8tbspn) vegetable oil

1 small aubergine, cut into 4cm (1½ inch) cubes

110g (4oz) button mushrooms, cut into quarters

2 large onions, cut into half and fairly thickly sliced

1 small green pepper, deseeded and diced

25ml (5tspn) Balti spice mix (see page 53)

150ml (¼pt) Balti sauce (see page 56)

15ml (1tbspn) Balti garam masala (see page 54)

1 Heat half the oil in a Balti pan, wok or large frying pan. Add the chilli and garlic and cook for a few minutes over a high heat. Now add the aubergine, mushrooms, onions and pepper and stir fry briskly for about 10 minutes until the vegetables are tender and browning. Remove from the oil with a slotted spoon.

2 Add the remaining oil to what is left in the pan. Stir in the Balti spice mix and cook for 2 minutes over a medium heat. Add the chicken and stir fry for 15 minutes, until just cooked.

3 Add the Balti sauce and simmer for 10 minutes.

4 Return the vegetables to the pan, add the garam masala and heat through for 5-10 minutes. Serve.

❖❖❖❖❖❖❖❖❖❖❖❖❖❖❖❖❖❖❖❖❖❖❖❖❖❖❖

Cook's tip

When dicing the vegetables, leave the aubergine until you are ready to cook it, as the cut surfaces discolour very quickly. Do not be tempted to drop it into water to try to prevent this - aubergine has a sponge-like quality and you will not achieve the browning when you stir fry. There is no need to peel the aubergine, in fact it would be a shame to remove that shiny purple skin, which also helps to hold the flesh together as the vegetable cooks.

❖❖❖❖❖❖❖❖❖❖❖❖❖❖❖❖❖❖❖❖❖❖❖❖❖❖❖

♣ DUCK BALTI ♣

A duck Balti is a real treat, so it is worth trying to find Barbary duck fillets for this dish. Their wonderful flavour combines with the spices and the orange particularly well.

SERVES: 4

PREPARATION TIME: 1 HOUR

700g (1½lb) duck fillets, cut into 3cm (1¼ inch) cubes

60ml (4tbspn) ghee or vegetable oil

2 onions, chopped

2 cloves garlic, crushed

2.5cm (1 inch) cube fresh root ginger, grated

1 fresh green chilli, chopped

10ml (2tspn) Balti spice mix (see page 53)

Finely grated zest of half an orange

Juice of 1 orange

2 small tomatoes, chopped

15ml (1tbspn) tomato purée

5ml (1tspn) dried fenugreek

5ml (1tspn) Balti garam masala (see page 54)

15ml (1tbspn) fresh coriander, chopped

1 Heat the ghee or oil in a Balti pan, wok or large frying pan over a medium to high heat. Add the onions, garlic and ginger and cook for about 5-10 minutes, until the onion is tinged brown.

2 Add the chilli and spice mix and cook for 2-3 minutes.

3 Add the duck and stir fry for about 5 minutes, until sealed on all sides. Add 150ml ('/₄pt) water and simmer, stirring often, for 15 minutes.

4 Add the orange zest and juice, tomatoes and tomato purée, fenugreek and garam masala. Simmer, stirring occasionally, for 25-30 minutes, until the duck is tender. Add more water if the mix becomes dry during cooking.

5 Sprinkle with coriander to serve.

❖❖❖❖❖❖❖❖❖❖❖❖❖❖❖❖❖❖❖❖❖❖❖❖❖

Cook's tip

Duck breast fillets are now available from most large super-markets. If you happen to have a whole duck that you would like to use in this dish, you can, of course, remove the fillets yourself. Follow the instructions given for chicken on page 68. You can use the carcass to make a stock that may be used to replace the water at stage 3 for an extra rich flavour.

❖❖❖❖❖❖❖❖❖❖❖❖❖❖❖❖❖❖❖❖❖❖❖❖❖

♣ CHICKEN BALTI WITH CREAM ♣ AND YOGHURT SAUCE

Only someone very economical with the truth could claim that the combination of chicken and yoghurt makes this a healthy dish. It is also full of nuts, cream and ghee, but the delicious flavours and texture make this a wonderful occasional treat.

Serves: 4

Preparation time: 35 minutes

700g (1½lb) boneless chicken breast, cut into 3cm (1¼ inch) cubes

60ml (4tbspn) ghee or vegetable oil

1 small onion, finely chopped

2 cloves garlic, crushed

5ml (1tspn) turmeric

2.5ml (½tspn) ground star anise (optional)

2.5ml (½tspn) ground cinnamon

150ml (¼pt) single cream

60ml (4tbspn) natural yoghurt

215ml (7½ fl oz) Balti sauce (see page 56)

110g (4oz) flaked almonds, toasted

15ml (1tbspn) fresh coriander, chopped

1 Heat 45ml (3tbspn) of the ghee or oil in a Balti pan, wok or large frying pan over a medium heat. Add the onion and garlic, and cook until golden - about 10 minutes.

2 Add the chicken breast and spices and stir fry for about 10 minutes.

3 Mix the yoghurt and cream. Add this to the pan with the Balti sauce

and 90g (3½oz) of the flaked almonds. Simmer gently for about 10-15 minutes until the chicken is cooked.

4 Stir in the coriander and heat for a few more minutes. Serve garnished with the remaining flaked almonds sizzled in the remaining melted ghee or oil.

Cook's tip

You can use your own homemade yoghurt in this recipe (see page 62) but the use of Greek yoghurt will make it even more rich and creamy.

✤ BALTI DRUMSTICKS ✤

This is a recipe specially developed to use drumsticks, or you could use a mixture of drumsticks and thighs. The sweetcorn adds texture to the sauce and also makes this a very colourful dish.

SERVES: 4

PREPARATION TIME: 50 MINUTES

8 small chicken drumsticks, skinned

30ml (2tbspn) ghee or vegetable oil

1 large onion, chopped

2 cloves garlic, crushed

3cm (1¼ inch) cube fresh root ginger, grated

150ml (¼pt) Balti sauce (see page 56)

1 small red pepper, seeded and diced

1 small green pepper, seeded and diced

1 small can sweetcorn, drained

15ml (1tbspn) Balti garam masala (see page 54)

1 Heat the ghee or oil in a Balti pan, wok or large frying pan over a medium heat. Add the onion, garlic and ginger and cook for 5-10 minutes until the onion is softened and just beginning to brown.

2 Add the chicken and cook for 10 minutes, turning from time to time, until it is lightly browned all round.

3 Add the Balti sauce, peppers and sweetcorn and simmer for 20 minutes.

4 Add the garam masala and simmer for a further 10 minutes. If the mix is becoming dry, add a little water, but the sauce should be quite

thick. Check that the chicken is cooked by piercing with a sharp knife. The meat should be tender and come away from the bone slightly, and any juices should be clear.

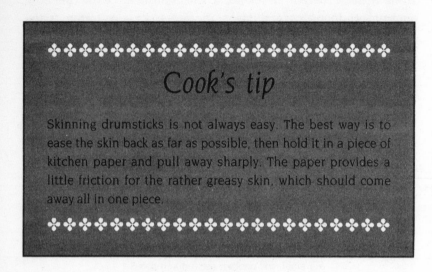

Cook's tip

Skinning drumsticks is not always easy. The best way is to ease the skin back as far as possible, then hold it in a piece of kitchen paper and pull away sharply. The paper provides a little friction for the rather greasy skin, which should come away all in one piece.

♣ CHICKEN AND EGG BALTI ♣

In this recipe it is not a question of which comes first - the chicken and egg are served together, wrapped in a creamy Balti sauce. For an extra special version, throw in a few peeled prawns when you add the eggs.

SERVES: 4

PREPARATION TIME: 35 MINUTES

450g (1lb) boneless chicken breast, cut into 3cm (1¼ inch) cubes

4 hard-boiled eggs, sliced in half lengthways

30ml (2tbspn) ghee or vegetable oil

1 onion, finely chopped

1 clove garlic, crushed

5cm (2 inch) cube fresh root ginger, grated

10ml (2tspn) Balti spice mix (see page 53)

5ml (1tspn) turmeric

30ml (2tbspn) ground almonds

400g (14oz) can chopped tomatoes

25g (1oz) coconut milk powder, mixed to a runny paste with water

15ml (1tbspn) fresh coriander, chopped

Toasted flaked almonds

1 Heat the ghee or oil in a Balti pan, wok or large frying pan over a medium heat. Add the onions and garlic and cook for about 10 minutes, until golden.

2 Add the chicken, ginger and spices and cook, stirring, for a further 10 minutes.

3 Add the almonds, tomatoes and coconut paste. Simmer for 15 minutes.

4 Add the coriander and eggs, keeping the yolks upwards. Simmer for a further 5 minutes and serve, sprinkled with flaked almonds.

♣ BALTI ROGAN JOSH ♣

"Rogan josh" suggests a dish cooked in a rich, red sauce. Often this is achieved by using food colours, but I prefer to use just about anything that is naturally red, as you will see from the recipe! This a very aromatic dish, using lots of spices.

SERVES: 4

PREPARATION TIME: 45 MINUTES

700g (1½lb) boneless chicken, cut into 3cm (1¼ inch) cubes

30ml (2tbspn) ghee or vegetable oil

1 small onion, finely chopped

2 cloves garlic, crushed

30ml (2tbspn) tandoori paste (see page 59)

2.5ml (½tspn) ground cloves

Pinch ground bay

2.5ml (½tspn) ground cinnamon

5ml (1tspn) ground cardamom

2.5ml (½tspn) ground cumin

2.5ml (½tspn) paprika

1 red chilli, chopped

275ml (½pt) Balti sauce (see page 56)

30ml (2tbspn) tomato purée

1 red pepper, deseeded and chopped

50g (2oz) fresh cooked beetroot, finely chopped

15ml (1tbspn) fresh coriander, chopped

1 Heat the ghee or oil in a Balti pan, wok or large frying pan over a medium heat. Add the onion and garlic and cook for 5 minutes until just starting to brown.

2 Add the chicken and stir fry for 10 minutes.

3 Add the tandoori paste, spices and red chilli and cook, stirring, for 2-3 minutes.

4 Add the Balti sauce and tomato purée with the red pepper and beetroot. Simmer for 20 minutes.

5 Stir in the coriander and cook for a further 5 minutes. Serve sprinkled with a little more fresh coriander.

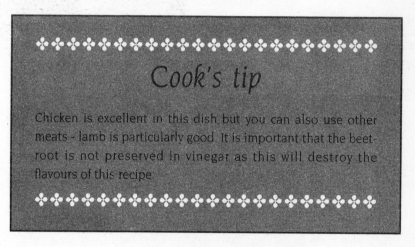

Cook's tip

Chicken is excellent in this dish but you can also use other meats - lamb is particularly good. It is important that the beetroot is not preserved in vinegar as this will destroy the flavours of this recipe.

♣ QUAIL BALTI ♣

It may seem strange to include a quail Balti dish, but it is probably one of the most authentic Balti meats. As quails are very small, it might look miserly to offer only one per portion, but two looks generous and probably means some will be left. This recipe solves the problem by halving the quails. You can then calculate three halves per guest.

SERVES: AT LEAST 4

PREPARATION TIME: 40 MINUTES

8 quails, skin on, cut in half lengthways

75ml (5tbspn) ghee or vegetable oil

2 small onions, chopped

3 cloves garlic, crushed

3cm (1¼ inch) cube fresh root ginger, grated

2 green chillies, finely chopped

4 tomatoes, skinned and chopped

25ml (5tspn) Balti spice mix (see page 53)

30ml (2tbspn) fresh coriander, chopped

5ml (1tspn) Balti garam masala

1 Heat the ghee or oil in a Balti pan, wok or large frying pan over a medium heat. Add the onions and garlic and cook for 10 minutes until golden brown.

2 Add the ginger, chillies and tomatoes and cook for 5 minutes, then add the Balti spice mix and a little water.

3 Add the quails and cook for 10 minutes, turning frequently.

4 Add about 60ml (4tbspn) of water, cover and simmer for 8-10 minutes. Stir in the coriander and serve, sprinkled with garam masala.

♣ BALTI STIR FRY ♣

All Balti dishes are stir fries to a certain extent, but this one combines elements of Chinese stir fry with Balti flavours to give a dish that is delicious and extremely quick to prepare. Vary the vegetables and poultry as much as you like: this is a recipe that would be good with chicken, turkey, duck or game. Given the possible permutations, it need never be the same twice!

SERVES: 4

PREPARATION TIME: 25 MINUTES

450g (1lb) boneless chicken breast, cut into thin strips

45ml (3tbspn) ghee or vegetable oil

2 large onions, halved and thinly sliced

1 clove garlic, crushed

1 green chilli, chopped

2.5cm (1 inch) cube fresh root ginger, grated

5ml (1tspn) Balti spice mix (see page 53)

1 green pepper, deseeded and finely sliced

1 large carrot, peeled and cut into matchsticks

2 sticks celery, thinly sliced

110g (4oz) white cabbage, shredded

50g (2oz) button mushrooms, sliced

50g (2oz) mangetout

90ml (6tbspn) Balti sauce (see page 56)

Fresh coriander leaves

1 Heat the ghee or oil in a Balti pan, wok or large frying pan over a medium to high heat. Add the onions and garlic and cook for 5

minutes. Add the green chilli, ginger and Balti spice mix and cook for a further 2 minutes.

2 Add the shredded chicken and stir fry for 5 minutes.

3 Add the vegetables to the pan and stir fry for a further 5-10 minutes, until the chicken is cooked and the vegetables still retain some crispness.

4 Pour over the Balti sauce, mix well and heat through for 2-3 minutes.

5 Serve, topped with whole coriander leaves.

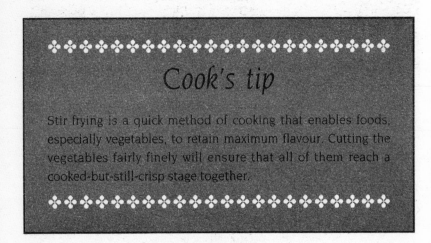

Cook's tip

Stir frying is a quick method of cooking that enables foods, especially vegetables, to retain maximum flavour. Cutting the vegetables fairly finely will ensure that all of them reach a cooked-but-still-crisp stage together.

MEAT

RECIPES

1 PAR-COOKED BALTI MEAT

A basic recipe to give you the basis of many Balti dishes

2 BASIC MEAT BALTI

Try this traditional recipe for your first Balti meat dish

3 BALTI PERSIAN STYLE

The addition of fruit and nuts provides the Persian influence in this lamb dish

4 BALTI TANDOORI

A great way to combine two classic flavours in one easy-to-cook dish

5 BALTI KEEMA

One of the quickest Balti recipes, which can be varied in many ways

6 LAMB AND CHICK PEA BALTI

A simple, delicious and very substantial Balti

7 MEATBALL BALTI

Spicy little meatballs cooked in a rich Balti sauce

8 BALTI KORMA

A mild, fragrant dish enriched with cream

9 MEAT AND CAULIFLOWER BALTI

An easy-to-prepare Balti, requiring no pre-mixes

10 SWEET AND SOUR BALTI

An interesting combination of flavours, which are absorbed by the potatoes

in this dish

11 BALTI DHANSAK

A Balti adaptation of a classic Indian dish, including lentils to add texture to the
sauce

12 MEAT AND SPINACH BALTI

Don't be put off by childhood memories of spinach - in a curry it is superb

This chapter includes a variety of meat Baltis, incorporating different types and cuts of meat. It is only possible to offer a selection of dishes here - in fact the possibilities are endless. You can extend your repertoire by mixing and matching your meats and recipes.

In India and Pakistan the choice of meat may be limited by religious laws. On the whole, Muslims do not eat pork and Hindus do not eat beef or veal. Christians are generally happy to eat either but in fact many people do not eat meat at all. It is perhaps not surprising that meat from sheep and goats is popular. Balti spices work well with these meats, but fortunately the Balti style of cooking can easily be adapted for use with beef, veal, pork, lamb, venison, rabbit and so forth.

As Balti is essentially a stir-frying technique, the final preparation and cooking is relatively quick. Because of this, many cuts of meat need to be partially cooked (par-cooked) before being added to the Balti. This also has the advantage of imparting some flavours into the meat before the final cooking. The traditional Balti method would involve a long, slow cooking over charcoal, which results in the meat slowly infusing in spices and becoming beautifully tender. However, most of us do not have hours to spare watching a gently simmering pot, even if we could muster the glowing charcoal embers. By par-cooking the meat, good flavour can be achieved, but in a quicker and more convenient way.

On the following pages you will find instructions for par-cooking larger cuts of meat, followed by recipes incorporating these. You will also find a number of recipes using minced meat, which can be added directly to the Balti pan without needing to be par-cooked.

BEEF

The quality of beef varies a great deal, depending not only on the age, breed and sex of the animal it comes from, but also on the way it is hung, stored and butchered. It is always a good idea to find a butcher whose style of meat you like and with whom you can discuss your requirements. When buying beef, choose meat that looks fresh and moist, though not with a lot of excess moisture. Ideally, the meat should have little flecks of fat throughout, known as marbling. Nowadays, many joints of meat are stripped of most of their natural fat and then additional fat is wrapped around. As you will almost certainly want to remove this before cooking, it is rather a waste.

Some butchers and supermarkets are now supplying Aberdeen Angus beef. This comes from animals reared on a special diet in a small part of Scotland and it is delicious. You might consider that the subtle flavour of this meat would be lost amongst the spices and seasonings of Balti, and since it carries a price premium, you may be wiser to look for good quality standard beef.

Quality is important because, even when the meat is par-cooked, the Balti cooking method will not give the meat a long, slow cooking that might render lower quality meat tender.

Sirloin may be sold on the bone or boneless. It is tender, full of flavour and excellent for use in Balti cookery. Trim off the excess fat prior to use. It is not necessary to par-cook this cut.

Fillet is the prime part of the carcass - the eye of the rib. It is generally sold as steaks. For a special occasion, it would make a wonderful Balti dish. There is certainly no need to par-cook this cut of meat. In fact, you may like to add it towards the end of cooking, so that it is actually slightly rare when served.

Brisket may be sold on or off the bone. A boneless joint gives ideal meat for par-cooking.

Rump is a large and tender cut of beef, from the hindquarters of the animal. You will usually find it sold in slices. If it is of good quality, it should not need par-cooking.

Topside is a very lean cut of meat, often sold with added fat. With this fat removed, it too makes an excellent meat for par-cooking.

Minced beef is available in a bewildering choice of forms at your supermarket or butcher's. The different kinds are usually divided into coarse or fine mince, and then sub-divided into fat levels. Mince traditionally was made from some of the poorer cuts of meat and tended to be high in fat. However, with the rise of interest in healthy eating, and with more and more people keen to reduce the fat level in their diets, you should be able to find mince with a fat level at least as low as 5%.

Frozen mince varies considerably in quality. Some economy minces include soya protein. However, if you find a good quality frozen mince, you will find that, even defrosted, it is very free-flowing. This makes it ideal for stir frying.

VEAL

Veal comes from young calves, so the meat is extremely lean and tender, fine-textured, pale pink and soft. Because the animal is so young, the connective tissues in the meat have not had a chance to develop and toughen the texture. This also means that there is very little fat. Almost any cut of veal would be ideal for Balti cookery, with the leg fillet and loin being particularly suitable.

Many people, of course, are not happy to eat veal, as they fear that the method of meat production is inhumane. To improve the colour and texture of the meat, calves are often allowed very little movement and are fed on milk. If you wish to buy veal, try to find a reputable supplier who has made sure that the animals have not been ill-treated.

LAMB

Lamb is a wonderfully tender meat and lends itself particularly well to Balti cookery. It can also be quite expensive, with cheaper cuts being rather fatty. It is usually sold on the bone, but a good butcher will remove this for you if you wish. The most expensive and arguably the best lamb is new-season British lamb. New Zealand lamb is cheaper.

and will almost certainly have been frozen. Lamb should have very little gristle, with a slight moistness to the meat.

Shoulder may be sold as a whole piece, or halved and sold as blade and knuckle, either bone-in or boned and rolled. This is ideal for par-cooking.

Noisettes are boned and rolled cutlets from the best end of neck. Diced, they can be used directly in a Balti recipe.

Leg, boned and rolled, is another cut that is ideal for par-cooking, particularly if you can find a really lean joint.

Diced lamb is available ready prepared and is ideal for Balti cookery. The meat usually comes from the shoulder, leg or chump.

Minced lamb is becoming much more widely available now, both fresh and frozen.

MUTTON

Once meat that formed a staple part of the diet in Britain, mutton is now rarely available. It is from an older animal than lamb, is less tender and usually requires a long, slow cooking. It is ideal for the kind of cooking done in Baltistan, but less useful for the adaptations that have become a feature of Balti cookery in this country.

PORK

Pork is available at excellent quality all year round. The lean pork should be pale pink and moist, with a slight marbling of fat. If the cut you have chosen has fat or skin, this should be removed prior to cooking. This is easy to do with a small, sharp knife.

Shoulder is a large joint that may well be divided into smaller cuts. Shoulder can also be cut into steaks.

Leg is also a large joint, which often comes divided into the fillet end and shank end, frequently boned and rolled. The fillet end is a prime joint for Balti cookery.

Loin may be sold boned and rolled as a joint, or cut into chops. The chops make ideal Balti meat, which doesn't need to be par-cooked.

Tenderloin is the tender, lean meat found just under the backbone of the loin. It is the pork equivalent to beef fillet and is sometimes sold as fillet, but should not be confused with the fillet end of the leg. It is a delicious, lean meat, which also does not require par-cooking.

Pork mince is another newcomer to supermarket shelves and is available both fresh and frozen. Alternatively, your butcher can prepare some for you. It can be used wherever mince is mentioned in a recipe.

GOAT

It is unlikely that you will find goat or kid meat unless you rear the animals yourself, but if you do have access to these meats, treat them as mutton or lamb.

VENISON

This meat is becoming much more readily available with the advent of venison farming. You will probably find it in a good butcher's or delicatessen. Or look in your local Yellow Pages as you may be surprised to find that there is a venison farm nearby. Venison benefits from par-cooking before being added to Balti dishes.

BUYING MEAT

Many people now buy their meat at their local supermarket with the rest of their groceries and may be tempted to believe that all that is available are the pre-wrapped plastic cartons of meat, but this is not always the case. Most supermarkets have a resident butcher. If you cannot find the cut you require, it is always worth asking if it can be prepared for you, while you complete the rest of your shopping. Also, many supermarkets now include a butcher's counter, rather like a butcher's shop within the store. It really is worth getting to know your butcher, whether in a high street store or supermarket, as you can then be sure of getting exactly the cut you want.

♣ PAR-COOKED BALTI MEAT ♣

The meat used in this recipe can be pork, beef, lamb, venison or rabbit. The cooking time can be adjusted according to the meat used.

MAKES: 12 PORTIONS

PREPARATION TIME: 30-50 MINUTES

2.2kg (5lb) meat, cut into 2.5cm (1 inch) cubes and trimmed of any gristle and excess fat

15ml (1tbspn) vegetable oil

2 onions, peeled and finely sliced

45ml (3tbspn) Balti garam masala (see page 54)

425ml (¾pt) stock or water

1 Preheat the oven to 190°C/375°F/Gas Mark 5.

2 In a large pan heat the oil and add the onion. Fry gently until soft.

3 Mix the garam masala with enough water to make a stiff paste. Add to the onions with the remaining water and bring to the boil. Add the meat and simmer for 5 minutes.

4 Transfer to a casserole with a tightly fitting lid and place in the oven for 20 minutes. Stir and return to the oven for a further 20 minutes.

5 Remove the meat from the stock and chill. Either use directly in a

recipe or freeze in batch sizes to suit your needs. The residual stock may also be frozen and incorporated into recipes.

COOKING TIMES

Use the following guide for cooking times, but remember to adjust them if you prefer your lamb pink or your beef rare. The times are for total cooking - always check the mix half way through cooking to ensure that there is enough liquid and to give an even cook to all pieces.

Remember that the meat will get an extra cooking time when you do

Lamb: 40 minutes

Beef: 30 minutes

Pork: 50 minutes

Venison: 50 minutes

Rabbit: 30 minutes

the final stir-frying. In the Balti area of Pakistan, meat would usually be pre-cooked on the bone. if you wish to do this, ask your butcher to cut the meat into pieces as small as possible - this usually involves the use of a meat cleaver and watching rather than performing is a less hazardous exercise. Remove any excess fat and gristle and cook as for boneless meat, extending the cooking time by 10 to 20 minutes depending on the size of the chunks. Once cooked and cooled, remove the meat from the bone.

✤ BASIC MEAT BALTI ✤

This makes a good starting point for the novice Balti cook. It will give you an idea of the flavours you can expect to achieve and, hopefully, whet your appetite to go on and try more adventurous recipes.

SERVES: 4

PREPARATION TIME: 40-50 MINUTES

450g (1lb) par-cooked meat

30ml (2tbspn) ghee or vegetable oil

4 cloves garlic, crushed

2 medium onions, peeled and finely sliced

75ml (5tbspn) Balti garam masala (see page 54)

75ml (4tbspn) vegetable oil

3 tomatoes, skinned and roughly chopped

200ml (⅓ pint) Balti stock (reserved from cooking the meat) or water

15ml (1tbspn) freshly chopped coriander

1 Heat the ghee or oil in a Balti pan, wok or large frying pan on a medium to high heat. Add the garlic and cook for 1-2 minutes.

2 Add the onion, reduce the heat to medium and cook, stirring, for about 8-10 minutes until the onion looks translucent and is just starting to brown on the edges.

3 Blend 60ml (4 tbspn) of the garam masala with the vegetable oil and enough water to make a stiff paste. Add the paste, meat and tomatoes to the onions in the pan and cook for a further 5 minutes, turning frequently until the spices are well dispersed.

4. Slowly mix in the stock or water and bring to the boil. Simmer for about 10 minutes, adding more liquid if necessary, until the meat is tender.

5 When the meat is cooked, sprinkle in the remaining garam masala and the coriander and mix well. Simmer for a further 10 minutes and serve.

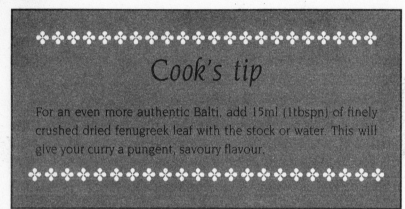

Cook's tip

For an even more authentic Balti, add 15ml (1tbspn) of finely crushed dried fenugreek leaf with the stock or water. This will give your curry a pungent, savoury flavour.

✤ BALTI PERSIAN STYLE ✤

Because of Baltistan's situation, there is a definite Persian influence on many Balti dishes. In this recipe it takes the form of dried fruit and nuts and a slightly sweet note.

SERVES: 4

PREPARATION TIME: 40-50 MINUTES

450g (1lb) par-cooked Balti meat - lamb is particularly good in this dish

30ml (2tbspn) ghee or vegetable oil

4 cloves garlic, peeled and crushed

2 medium onions, peeled and finely chopped

60ml (4tbspn) Balti spice mix (see page 53)

120g (4oz) dried apricots

120g (4oz) dates, chopped

60ml (4tbspn) pine kernels

300ml (12 fl oz) Balti sauce (see page 56)

15ml (1tbspn) freshly chopped coriander

1 Heat the ghee or oil in a Balti pan, wok or large frying pan over a medium to high heat. Add the garlic, onion and spice mix and cook for about 10 minutes until the onion is soft and just beginning to brown.

2 Add the meat and cook for 5 minutes.

3 Add the fruit, pine kernels and Balti sauce. Simmer, stirring occasionally, for about 10 minutes.

4 Add a little water if dry, then add the coriander, simmer for 10 minutes and serve.

❖ BALTI TANDOORI ❖

In this recipe two great curry tastes are combined in one marvellous dish. I have used tandoori lamb here, but the recipe would be equally delicious made with chicken or fish.

SERVES: 4

PREPARATION TIME: 40 MINUTES

450g (1lb) tandoori lamb (see page 61)

30ml (2tbspn) ghee or vegetable oil

2 large onions, thinly sliced

3 cloves garlic, crushed

½ green pepper, deseeded and chopped

300ml (12 fl oz) Balti sauce (see page 56)

15ml (1tbspn) Balti garam masala (see page 54)

15ml (1tbspn) finely chopped coriander

1 Heat the ghee or oil in a Balti pan, wok or large frying pan over a medium heat. Add the onion and garlic and cook for 10 minutes until the onion is soft and tinged brown.

2 Add the green pepper and lamb and stir fry for about 10 minutes.

3 Add the Balti sauce and simmer for 10 minutes, adding a little water if the mixture starts to become dry.

4 Add the garam masala and coriander and cook for a further 5-10 minutes. Serve.

♣ BALTI KEEMA ♣

When using mince, there is no need to par-cook the meat. I have found that using frozen, free-flowing mince, defrosted, makes stir frying much easier - with less risk of producing a giant Balti burger! Peas are a classic addition to this dish, but diced tomatoes, chopped peppers or lentils would also be delicious. Minced beef is a good choice, but there is now quite a variety of minced meats available, including lamb, turkey and pork, so do experiment - the dish will be different every time.

SERVES: 4

PREPARATION TIME: 35 MINUTES

700g (1½lb) minced meat, defrosted if frozen

30ml (2tbspn) ghee or vegetable oil

3 cloves garlic, crushed

2 large onions, peeled and chopped

45ml (3tbspn) Balti garam masala (see page 54)

225g (8oz) frozen peas

30ml (2tbspn) tomato purée

15ml (1tbspn) coriander, finely chopped

1 Heat the ghee or oil in a Balti pan, wok or frying pan over a medium heat. Add the garlic and onions and cook for about 10 minutes until golden brown.

2 Add the mince and cook for 20 minutes, stirring frequently.

3 Mix the garam masala with enough water to make a thick paste. Add this, the peas and the tomato purée and simmer for a further 10 minutes, adding a little water if the mixture becomes too dry.

4 Add the coriander and heat for 2-3 minutes. Serve.

♣ LAMB AND CHICK PEA BALTI ♣

Canned chick peas make this a very speedy and substantial dish. You can, of course, cook your own chick peas (see page 147) but in this recipe you really cannot tell the difference between home-cooked and canned. This is a hearty dish, so serve with a simple bread.

SERVES: 4

PREPARATION TIME: 45 MINUTES

700g (1½lb) minced lamb, defrosted if frozen

440g (15½oz) can chick peas. drained

60ml (4tbspn) ghee or vegetable oil

2 large onions, finely chopped

4 cloves garlic, crushed

1 small green pepper, deseeded and chopped

1 fresh green chilli, finely chopped

2 tomatoes, skinned and chopped

25ml (5tspn) Balti spice mix (see page 53)

4cm (1½ inch) cube fresh root ginger, grated

150ml (¼pt) Balti sauce (see page 56)

2.5ml (½tspn) salt

Pinch of ground black pepper

15ml (1tbspn) fresh coriander, finely chopped

1 Heat the ghee or oil in a Balti pan, wok or large frying pan over a medium heat. Add the onions and garlic and cook until golden.

2 Add the lamb and cook, stirring well, until it begins to brown. Add the green pepper, chilli, tomatoes and spice mix and cook, stirring, for 5 minutes.

3 Add 150ml (¼pt) of water and bring to the boil. Stir in the ginger and Balti sauce, turn the heat low and simmer for 20 minutes, adding a little more water if the mixture starts to look dry.

4 Add the chick peas, salt, pepper and coriander and cook for a further 5 minutes before serving.

Cook's tip

You can vary this dish by using red kidney beans or butter beans in place of the chick peas.

♣ MEATBALL BALTI ♣

Koftas, Indian meatballs, are delicious balls of spiced minced meat. These are often popular with children (perhaps with the chillies omitted) and are usually made with lamb, but you can used minced beef if you prefer. As beef lacks the sweetness of lamb, add 15ml (1tbspn) of tomato purée to the meat mix before forming into balls.

SERVES: 4

PREPARATION TIME: 45 MINUTES

450g (1lb) minced lamb

2 medium onions, chopped as finely as possible

1 clove garlic, crushed

2 green chillies, finely chopped

5ml (1tspn) fresh coriander, finely chopped

2.5ml (½tspn) ground ginger

2.5ml (½tspn) paprika

60ml (4tbspn) ghee or vegetable oil

10ml (2tspn) Balti spice mix (see page 53)

300ml (½pt) Balti sauce (see page 56)

2.5cm (1 inch) cube fresh root ginger, grated

1 Mix together the minced lamb, onions, garlic, chillies, coriander and spices. Form into balls, about 2.5cm (1 inch) in diameter.

2 Heat the ghee or oil in a Balti pan, wok or large frying pan over a medium to high heat. Add the meatballs and cook, turning frequently, until well browned. Add the Balti spice mix, Balti sauce and ginger, and mix together gently.

3 Reduce the heat and simmer on a medium heat for 15-20 minutes. Serve.

❖ BALTI KORMA ❖

Korma will be familiar to those who visit Indian restaurants. It has come to describe a mild, creamy sauce with nuts. This recipe combines a korma sauce with Balti seasoning to give a dish with a delicate flavour and just a touch of background heat.

SERVES: 4

PREPARATION TIME: 30 MINUTES

450g (1lb) par-cooked meat

30ml (2tbspn) ghee or vegetable oil

1 large onion, finely sliced

3 cloves garlic, crushed

10ml (2tspn) Balti spice mix (see page 53)

2.5ml ($^1/_2$tspn) turmeric

300ml ($^1/_2$pt) Balti sauce (see page 56)

150ml ($^1/_4$ pt) double cream

50g (2oz) flaked almonds, toasted

15ml (1tbspn) fresh coriander, roughly chopped

1 Heat the ghee or oil in a Balti pan, wok or large frying pan over a medium heat. Add the onion and garlic and cook for 10 minutes until beginning to brown.

2 Add the par-cooked meat, Balti spice mix and turmeric, and cook, stirring, for 5 minutes.

3 Add the Balti sauce and simmer for 10 minutes.

4 Stir in the cream and almonds and simmer gently for a further 5 minutes. Stir in the coriander and serve.

✤ MEAT AND CAULIFLOWER BALTI ✤

This is a particularly easy curry, despite the length of the ingredient list, because it does not require any pre-mixes. This makes it a good Balti for beginners and may inspire you to make Balti garam masala and spice mix for other recipes.

SERVES: 4

PREPARATION TIME: 45 MINUTES

450g (1lb) minced meat

1 small cauliflower, cut into small florets with thicker stalks discarded

45ml (3tbspn) ghee or vegetable oil

1 large onion, finely chopped

5ml (1tspn) cardamom seeds, crushed

2.5ml (½tspn) ground cinnamon

2.5cm (1 inch) cube fresh root ginger, grated

2 cloves garlic, crushed

2.5ml (½tspn) turmeric

5ml (1tspn) chilli powder

5ml (1tspn) ground cumin

30ml (2tbspn) tomato purée

150ml (¼pt) natural yoghurt

Pinch of salt

15ml (1tbspn) coriander, roughly chopped

1 Heat the ghee or oil in a Balti pan, wok or large frying pan and add the onion. Cook over a medium heat until softened and golden.

2 Add the cardamom seeds, cinnamon, ginger, garlic, turmeric, chilli powder and cumin. Mix well and cook for 4-5 minutes.

3 Add the mince and tomato purée and cook for 20 minutes, stirring until the meat begins to brown. Add the yoghurt and 150ml (¼pt) of water. Bring to the boil.

4 Add the cauliflower florets and reduce the heat to low. Simmer for 20 minutes, stirring occasionally until the cauliflower is tender. Add more water if necessary.

5 Add salt to taste. Sprinkle with coriander and serve.

Cook's tip

If you don't have any tomato purée, use fresh, peeled tomatoes, finely chopped, instead. You will need three or four in this recipe.

♣ SWEET AND SOUR BALTI ♣

In this recipe the sweetness of tomatoes, fried onions and a little sugar contrasts with the sharpness of yoghurt, lemon juice and fenugreek leaves to give an interesting combination.

SERVES: 4

PREPARATION TIME: 50 MINUTES

450g (1lb) par-cooked meat

60ml (4tbspn) ghee or vegetable oil

2 onions, finely chopped

2 cloves garlic, crushed

1 green chilli, chopped

2.5cm (1 inch) cube fresh root ginger, grated

30ml (2tbspn) tomato purée

5ml (1tspn) Balti garam masala (see page 54)

5ml (1tspn) chilli powder

2.5ml (½tspn) paprika

150ml (¼pt) stock or water

225g (8oz) potatoes, peeled and cut into 1cm (½ inch) cubes

15ml (1tbspn) sugar

5ml (1tspn) dried fenugreek leaves, crushed

150ml (¼pt) natural yoghurt

30ml (2tbspn) lemon juice

1 Heat the ghee or oil in a Balti pan, wok or large frying pan over a medium heat. Add the onions, garlic, chilli and ginger and cook, turning occasionally, until the onion is softened and golden.

2 Add the tomato purée, garam masala, chilli powder and paprika and cook, stirring all the time, for 3-4 minutes.

3 Add the meat and stock or water and cook for 15 minutes.

4 Add the potatoes and cook for a further 15 minutes until they are tender but not soft. Add more stock or water if the mixture becomes too dry.

5 Mix the yoghurt with the sugar and fenugreek and stir into the Balti. Stir gently for 4-5 minutes to heat through.

6 Turn into a serving dish, sprinkle with lemon juice and serve.

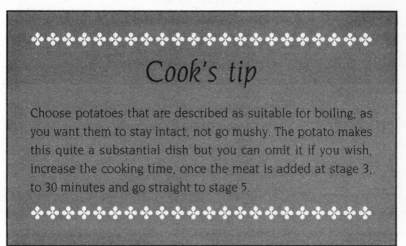

Cook's tip

Choose potatoes that are described as suitable for boiling, as you want them to stay intact, not go mushy. The potato makes this quite a substantial dish but you can omit it if you wish, increase the cooking time, once the meat is added at stage 3, to 30 minutes and go straight to stage 5.

♣ BALTI DHANSAK ♣

This Balti dish is an adaptation of one found in all Indian restaurants. The lentils add texture and thickness to the sauce and are vital to the recipe. If you do not like lentils, this one is not for you - there are no substitutes!

SERVES: 4

PREPARATION TIME: 45 MINUTES + COOKING TIME FOR LENTILS

450g (1lb) par-cooked meat

225g (½lb) red lentils, pre-cooked (see page 147)

30ml (2tbspn) ghee or vegetable oil

1 large onion, finely chopped

2 cloves garlic, crushed

5ml (1tspn) fenugreek seeds

5ml (1tspn) cumin seeds

200g (7oz) canned chopped tomatoes in natural juice

300ml (½pt) Balti sauce (see page 56)

15ml (1tbspn) granulated sugar

15ml (1tbspn) lemon juice

15ml (1tbspn) Balti garam masala (see page 54)

Salt and chilli powder to taste

15ml (1tbspn) fresh coriander, finely chopped

1 Heat the ghee or oil in a Balti pan, wok or large frying pan over a medium heat. Add the onion, garlic, fenugreek seeds and cumin seeds and fry, stirring, for about 10 minutes until golden.

2 Add the meat and cook for 5 minutes. Stir in the tomatoes and Balti sauce and simmer for a further 10 minutes.

3 Add the lentils, sugar, lemon juice and garam masala, and chilli powder and salt to taste. Simmer for about 15 minutes, adding some water if the sauce becomes too dry - it should have a thick, creamy consistency at the end of the cooking time.

4 Stir in the coriander and serve.

♣ MEAT AND SPINACH BALTI ♣

The spinach in this dish adds a rich flavour and colour to the Balti. The recipe calls for some whole spices - these are not intended to be eaten. If you cannot trust your family or guests to remove them for themselves, take them out before serving this dish. I find that counting them in and counting them out ensures that nobody chokes on a whole clove!

SERVES: 4

PREPARATION TIME: 40 MINUTES

450g (1lb) par-cooked meat - beef or lamb works well

450g (1lb) frozen chopped spinach, defrosted, retain liquid

60ml (4tbspn) ghee or vegetable oil

4 whole cloves

1 bay leaf

4 cardamom pods

1 large onion, finely chopped

3 cloves garlic, crushed

2.5cm (1 inch) fresh root ginger, grated

10ml (2tspn) Balti spice mix (see page 53)

45ml (3tbspn) natural yoghurt

2.5ml (½tspn) Balti garam masala (see page 54)

1 Heat the ghee or oil in a Balti pan, wok or large frying pan over a medium heat. Add the cloves, bay leaf and cardamom pods and cook, stirring, for a few seconds. Quickly add the onion, garlic and ginger and cook for about 10 minutes, stirring from time to time, until the onion starts to brown.

2 Stir in the Balti spice mix and cook for 1 minute.

3 Add the meat and cook for 5 minutes.

4 Slowly stir in the yoghurt until thoroughly incorporated, by which time the meat should be starting to brown.

5 Add the spinach and mix well. Simmer for 10 minutes. Add the garam masala and cook for a further 10 minutes. By this time the sauce should be thick and green. Remove the whole spices and serve.

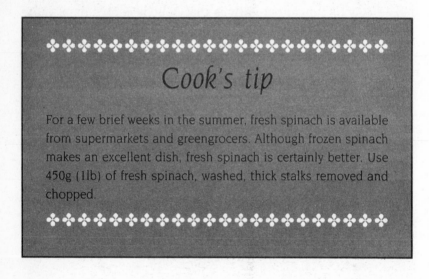

Cook's tip

For a few brief weeks in the summer, fresh spinach is available from supermarkets and greengrocers. Although frozen spinach makes an excellent dish, fresh spinach is certainly better. Use 450g (1lb) of fresh spinach, washed, thick stalks removed and chopped.

FISH AND SHELLFISH

RECIPES

1 BASIC FISH BALTI

Your fish Balti starting point

2 BALTI PRAWNS

A quick and delicious recipe for prawns of any size

3 SMOKED FISH BALTI

A Balti with a wonderfully intense flavour

4 SARDINE BALTI

Fresh sardines make this a specially tasty recipe

5 BALTI SPICED PRAWNS WITH PEAS

A hot and spicy Balti classic

6 FISH AND TOMATO BALTI

A simple but succulent fish Balti

7 OYSTER BALTI

A luxurious dish in which subtle spicing enhances the delicate

flavour of the oysters

8 KASHMIRI FISH BALTI

A rich fish Balti with a creamy, nutty sauce

Baltistan is a long way from the sea, but it does enjoy the advantage of numerous lakes and streams and the Indus River. Therefore there is no shortage of freshwater fish and shellfish. Fortunately recipes can easily be adapted to suit the fish available in your area.

Sadly there has been a steady decline in the number of high street wet fish shops, although this has been paralleled, probably not by coincidence, with the advent of fresh fish counters in many supermarkets. You may well find your local market has a fish stall, and if you live near the coast you probably have a favourite place to buy fish very nearly direct from the boats.

Strangely, for a nation with a great seafaring tradition, the British are not great fish eaters, unless it comes surrounded in crisp batter and accompanied by a mound of chips! Balti cooking and fish make a great partnership and if you take a look at your supermarket's fish counter you will see there is a huge range to choose from - not only locally caught fish, but also more exotic varieties. Do not be afraid to ask your fishmonger's advice - he or she will be happy to discuss with you the fish best suited to your requirements.

Fish is also a remarkably healthy choice. White fish contains very little fat, and oily fish, although, as its name suggests, higher in fat, contains the polyunsaturated type and is rich in vitamins A, D and particularly E.

On the following pages you will find a basic outline of the types of fish available followed by some recipes including them. However, as I have said with meat and poultry, the fish suggested in the recipe is only a guide - the choice is yours. As usual, there is a basic recipe to begin, with more adventurous recipes to follow.

WHITE FISH

This group includes some of the most popular fish, which vary hugely in size. The larger types, such as cod, haddock, coley and hake are usually sold as steaks and for Baltis they are best off the bone. Other useful fish in this category are monkfish, halibut and turbot. The flesh of these fish is firmer and some describe turbot as having an almost meaty texture. This characteristic makes these fish particularly suitable for Balti dishes, as the flesh is less likely to fall apart when cooked. They tend not to be the cheapest available, but a Balti is a good way of stretching a little fish to feed several people. The smaller types of white fish are often sold as fillets. Popular examples include such easily available fish as plaice, sole and whiting.

OILY FISH

This group includes herring and other members of the same family, such as pilchards, sardines and sprats. Mackerel and whitebait also fall into this category. These fish are usually sold whole - there's probably not a great demand for tiny filleted whitebait!

FRESHWATER FISH

A lot of freshwater fish, such as carp, perch and pike, are edible but not often eaten. However, this family also includes salmon and trout, which are becoming increasingly popular. The farming of both salmon and trout has made these fish much more accessible and considerably cheaper in the past few years. In fact farmed salmon is now less expensive than cod. Purists would doubtless argue that farmed salmon lacks the flavour of that caught in the wild, but when cooked by the Balti method this is really not a problem. Salmon is usually sold as steaks or fillets, but look out for offers on whole fish too; sometimes these are real bargains.

EXOTIC FISH

There are literally thousands of types of fish, with new ones appearing on the fishmonger's stall all the time. These newcomers tend to be noticeable because of their colours and shapes. Shark, swordfish and tuna are particularly useful for the stir-frying cooking method as they hold together well. They are usually sold as steaks. I would not advocate snapping up a bargain by buying the whole fish, unless you have a very large freezer!

SHELLFISH

This group can be divided into three:

1 Molluscs are protected by a strong shell - either single or hinged - and include whelks, winkles, mussels, oysters and scallops. They are totally interchangeable in Balti recipes.

2 Crustaceans have a skeleton and shell, which varies in toughness from the hefty armour of a lobster to the soft shell of a shrimp. In between we find crabs, crayfish and prawns of various sizes.

3 Cephalopods are shellfish with no shell - octopus and squid are the most common varieties.

SMOKED FISH

Smoking has been used as a form of preservation since ancient times. Some smoked fish, such as kippers, have such a strong and individual taste that they are best simply cooked and served, but others, including smoked cod and haddock, readily lend themselves to Balti recipes.

Smoked shellfish, particularly mussels and oysters, are delicious. Unless you are lucky enough to live near a fish-smoker (you will find some addresses at the back of the book), these will probably only be available to you canned in oil. They still provide a wonderful twist to a basic fish Balti if you add a few towards the end of the cooking time.

CANNED FISH

Many kinds of fish are now available tinned in brine. Mackerel and tuna are fine subjects for a Balti. Choose cans labelled as steaks or chunks as you want the pieces to be as large as possible. Always drain well and remember you may have to adjust the seasoning in your recipe to allow for the salt in the brine.

REMEMBER...

Your fishmonger is there to clean, skin and fillet fish, and unless you are a whiz with a filleting knife, it's probably more economical to leave these jobs to an expert. But do ask for the trimmings if you want to make fish stock.

The other point to keep in mind when serving Balti fish dishes is that there is always a risk the fish may contain some bones, however careful you have been. It is probably wise to warn your fellow eaters of this.

♣ BASIC FISH BALTI ♣

This recipe provides your fish Balti starting point. It has a medium heat and really can be made with any type of fish. Unless you are using a particularly firm fish, it is better to cook it whole and cut into cubes before serving so that it does not break up during cooking.

SERVES: 4

PREPARATION TIME: 40 MINUTES

700g (1½lb) any type of fish fillets or steaks

45ml (3tbspn) ghee or vegetable oil

2 small onions, finely chopped

3 cloves garlic, crushed

1 green chilli, finely chopped

15ml (1tbspn) Balti garam masala (see page 54)

150ml (¼pt) milk

15ml (1tbspn) fresh coriander, finely chopped

Pinch of Balti garam masala (see page 54)

1 Heat 30ml (2tbspn) of the ghee or oil in a Balti pan, wok or large frying pan over a medium heat. Add the onion and garlic and cook for about 10 minutes until softened and beginning to brown.

2 Mix the garam masala with the remaining ghee (melted) or oil and enough water to make a stiff paste. Add the green chilli, garam masala paste and fish to the pan and gently stir fry for 5-10 minutes.

3 Gradually add the milk, stirring carefully, and simmer over a low heat for a further 10 minutes. Check that the fish is cooked, then carefully remove it using a fish slice or large slotted spoon and cut it into bite-sized chunks. Return to the pan with the coriander and heat through.

4 Serve sprinkled with a little garam masala.

✤ BALTI PRAWNS ✤

Prawns are always popular in curries and quite often the only fish you will find on an Indian restaurant menu. They lend themselves particularly well to the quick stir-frying technique of Balti cookery. Use cooked prawns of any size.

SERVES: 4

PREPARATION TIME: 20 MINUTES

700g (1½lb) prawns, weighed after defrosting and draining if frozen

30ml (2tbspn) ghee or vegetable oil

1 onion, finely chopped

1 clove garlic, crushed

1 green chilli, chopped

2.5cm (1inch) cube fresh root ginger, grated

10ml (2tspn) Balti spice mix (see page 53)

1 green pepper, deseeded and cut into small dice

10ml (2tspn) Balti garam masala (see page 54)

15ml (1tbspn) fresh coriander, chopped

1 Heat the ghee or oil in a Balti pan, wok or large frying pan over a medium heat. Add the onion and garlic and cook for 5 minutes.

2 Add the chilli, ginger and spice mix and cook for a further 5 minutes.

3 Add the prawns and green pepper and stir fry for about 5 minutes, adding a little water to stop the mixture sticking if necessary.

4 Stir in the garam masala and coriander and cook for a further 5 minutes, adding a little more water if necessary, but the mixture should be quite dry. Serve.

♣ SMOKED FISH BALTI ♣

Smoked fish gives a Balti a wonderfully intense flavour. By soaking the fish in the milk, the smokiness is imparted to the sauce. Smoked fish is a little more robust than its unsmoked counterparts, so cut the fish into chunks before beginning the recipe.

SERVES: 4

PREPARATION TIME: 30 MINUTES + 1 HOUR SOAKING TIME

700g (1½lb) smoked haddock or cod

150ml (¼pt) milk

45ml (3tbspn) ghee or vegetable oil

2.5ml (½tspn) cumin seeds

2 large onions, finely chopped

3 cloves garlic, crushed

15ml (1tbspn) Balti garam masala (see page 54)

150ml (5 fl oz) natural Greek yoghurt

15ml (1tbspn) fresh coriander, chopped

1 Cut the fish into 5cm (2 inch) cubes. Cover with the milk and leave to soak for an hour.

2 Heat 30ml (2tbspn) of the ghee or oil in a Balti pan, wok or large frying pan over a medium heat. Add the cumin seeds and fry for 30 seconds before adding the onion and garlic. Cook for about 10 minutes until golden brown.

3 Mix the garam masala with the remaining ghee (melted) or oil and enough water to form a thickish paste. Stir the paste and the yoghurt into the pan. Once mixed and sizzling, add the fish and milk. Cook

briskly for 5 minutes, then reduce the heat and simmer gently for 10 minutes or until the fish is cooked. It should flake apart when gently pressed.

4 Stir in the coriander, heat through and serve.

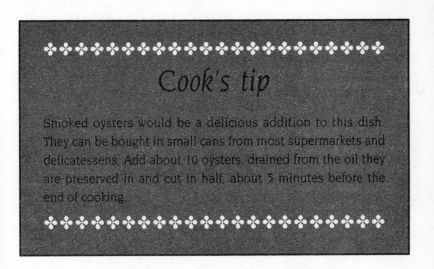

Cook's tip

Smoked oysters would be a delicious addition to this dish. They can be bought in small cans from most supermarkets and delicatessens. Add about 10 oysters, drained from the oil they are preserved in and cut in half, about 5 minutes before the end of cooking.

♣ SARDINE BALTI ♣

This dish could also be made with whitebait or pilchards, but fresh sardines are now readily available and are particularly delicious.

SERVES: 4

PREPARATION TIME: 30 MINUTES

450g (1lb) fresh sardines

45ml (3tbspn) ghee or vegetable oil

1 onion, finely chopped

1 clove garlic, crushed

2.5cm (1 inch) cube fresh root ginger, grated

1 green chilli, chopped

15ml (1tbspn) coconut milk powder, mixed to a thickish paste with water

150ml (¼pt) Balti sauce (see page 56)

15ml (1tbspn) fresh coriander, chopped

1 Heat the ghee or oil in a Balti pan, wok or large frying pan over a medium heat. Add the onion and garlic and cook for 10 minutes until softened and just beginning to brown.

2 Add the ginger and chilli and cook for 2-3 minutes.

3 Add the sardines and stir fry for 5 minutes.

4 Stir in the coconut paste and Balti sauce and simmer for a further 10 minutes.

5 Serve, sprinkled with coriander.

✤ BALTI SPICED PRAWNS WITH PEAS ✤

This is quite a hot dish, so reduce the number of green chillies if you prefer a milder version. If the prawns are frozen, defrost and drain them before weighing them for this recipe.

SERVES: 4

PREPARATION TIME: 30 MINUTES

45og (1lb) prawns

45ml (3tbspn) ghee or vegetable oil

2 small onions, finely chopped

4 cloves garlic, crushed

4 green chillies, chopped

2.5ml (½tspn) turmeric

10ml (2tbspn) Balti spice mix (see page 53)

Pinch of salt

150g (5oz) peas

5ml (1tspn) brown sugar

30ml (2tbspn) fresh coriander, chopped

1 Heat the ghee or oil in a Balti pan, wok or large frying pan over a medium heat. Add the onion and garlic and cook for 5 minutes. Add the chilli, turmeric and spice mix and cook for a further 5 minutes.

2 Add the prawns to the pan with a little water and simmer for 10 minutes.

3 Add the peas and sugar and cook for a further 5 minutes, adding a little more water to make a fairly thick sauce.

4 Add half the coriander and cook for 2-3 minutes. Sprinkle with the rest of the coriander and serve.

♣ FISH AND TOMATO BALTI ♣

In this recipe you have a choice - you can either pre-cook the fish, then dice it and add it towards the end of cooking, or you can cook it all the way through in the Balti, as in the method described. The fish will flake, but this simply gives the Balti a different texture.

SERVES: 4

PREPARATION TIME: 30 MINUTES

700g (1½lb) white fish, cut into 2.5cm (1 inch) cubes

30ml (2tbspn) ghee or vegetable oil

2 onions, chopped

3 cloves garlic, crushed

2.5cm (1 inch) cube fresh root ginger, grated

15ml (1tbspn) Balti spice mix (see page 53)

400g (14oz) can chopped tomatoes

5ml (1tspn) Balti garam masala (see page 54)

15ml (1tbspn) fresh coriander, chopped

1 Heat the ghee or oil in a Balti pan, wok or large frying pan over a medium heat. Add the onions and garlic and cook for 10 minutes until soft and golden.

2 Add the ginger and spice mix and cook for a further 2 or 3 minutes. Add the fish pieces and fry gently for 5 minutes.

3 Add the tomatoes and bring to the boil. Now lower the heat and simmer gently for 10 minutes until the fish is cooked.

4 Stir in the garam masala and coriander and heat through. Serve.

♣ OYSTER BALTI ♣

This is a simple but luxurious dish. The ingredients are kept to a minimum so that the flavour of the oysters is not masked but gently enhanced by the coriander. This is one of the few recipes in this book that serves 2 rather than 4, for two reasons. Firstly, oysters are wickedly expensive, and you may only want to buy enough for yourself and your nearest and dearest. Secondly, given the near legendary powers of oysters, you may simply not want anyone else around!

SERVES: 2

PREPARATION TIME: 12 MINUTES

12 oysters, shelled

30ml (2tbspn) ghee or vegetable oil

2 tomatoes, skinned and chopped

1 clove garlic, crushed

30ml (2tbspn) fresh coriander, chopped

150ml (¼pt) Balti sauce (see page 56)

Pinch of Balti garam masala (see page 54)

1 Heat the ghee or oil in a Balti pan, wok or frying pan over a medium heat. Add the tomatoes, garlic and half the coriander and cook for 5 minutes.

2 Add the Balti sauce and simmer for 2-3 minutes.

3 Add the oysters and cook, stirring continuously, for a further 2-3 minutes.

4 Serve, sprinkled with garam masala and the remaining coriander.

♣ KASHMIRI FISH BALTI ♣

A rich fish Balti, this dish has a creamy, nutty sauce, aromatic with herbs and spices. It is particularly good made with salmon or trout, but any fish works in this sauce. The dish requires no pre-mixes.

SERVES: 4

PREPARATION TIME: 25 MINUTES

700g (1½lb) fish, cut into 5cm (2¼ inch) cubes

15ml (1tbspn) ghee or vegetable oil

5ml (1tspn) cumin seeds

2.5ml (½tspn) turmeric

2.5ml (½tspn) coriander seeds, lightly crushed

Pinch each of ground cloves, ground bay leaves and ground cinnamon

1 green chilli, finely chopped

3cm (1¼ inch) cube fresh root ginger, grated

150ml (¼pt) natural Greek yoghurt

150ml (¼pt) single cream

30ml (2tbspn) ground almonds

15ml (1tbspn) fresh coriander, chopped

15ml (1tbspn) fresh parsley, chopped

1 Heat the ghee or oil in a Balti pan, wok or large frying pan over a medium to high heat. Add the dry spices and cook, stirring, for 30 seconds.

2 Add the chilli and ginger and cook, stirring, for a further 2 minutes. Stir in the yoghurt and bring to a simmer, then add the fish and cream and cook gently for 15 minutes until the fish is cooked.

3 Stir in the almonds and herbs and cook for a further 5 minutes. Serve.

VEGETABLES

RECIPES

1 MIXED VEGETABLE BALTI

A basic Balti to serve as an accompaniment or a main dish

2 DRY LENTIL BALTI

A substantial lentil dish with a creamy texture

3 POTATO BALTI

Potatoes absorb the aromatic spices in this versatile recipe

4 OKRA BALTI

A delicious Balti treatment of this unusual vegetable

5 SPICY SWEETCORN BALTI

Sweetcorn makes this dish as colourful as it is tasty

6 SPICY AUBERGINE BALTI

The rich sauce of this recipe makes it ideal for serving with a dry Balti

7 CHICK PEA AND MUSHROOM BALTI

Chilli gives warmth to this hearty dish

8 KIDNEY BEAN BALTI

This recipe brings out the delicious, nutty taste of red kidney beans

9 MUSHROOM AND PEA BALTI

Mushrooms absorb the spiciness of Balti particularly well

in this recipe

10 BLACK EYED BEAN, SPINACH AND MUSHROOM BALTI

Spinach adds a richness to this combination dish

11 SWEETCORN AND POTATO BALTI

One of my favourites - a really comforting dish!

12 BALTI CARROTS, PEAS AND POTATOES

A mixed vegetable dish that is a meal in itself

13 SPICY GREEN BEAN BALTI

This vegetable dish makes a wonderful accompaniment to

heavier meat dishes

14 MUSHROOM AND RED PEPPER BALTI

A quick and easy vegetable dish to accompany cold meats

or any Balti main course

egetables can be used in three ways in Balti dishes. Firstly, you can par-cook the vegetable of your choice separately and then add it to your favourite meat or fish Balti to form part of the dish. Secondly, you can make a small vegetable Balti to accompany your main dish. Finally, whether you are a vegetarian or not, a large Balti containing pulses and vegetables makes a delicious main-course dish.

You already know that one of the joys of Balti is the way that different dishes can be combined. In the same way, there is no end to the possible combinations of vegetables with vegetables, meat or fish.

On the following pages, you will find suggestions for vegetables that can be par-cooked and added to other dishes. Then there's a look at preparing dried legumes, such as lentils and split peas. While most vegetables can be prepared in small quantities, I would suggest that you cook legumes in bulk, as they need quite a long cooking time. You can then freeze them in convenient batches. Of course, if you feel that life is too short to boil a chick pea, there are always canned legumes readily available.

The last part of this section contains recipes for more hearty vegetable Baltis. These recipes are for smaller amounts than other recipes in this book, so that you can use them as side dishes. Alternatively, they will serve two people as a main meal, so you can always multiply the amounts if you wish to serve more people.

The times given for cooking vegetables can only be a guide. Individual tastes vary quite a lot. Bear in mind that if a vegetable can be eaten raw, a very short par-cooking time is probably all that's needed, as such a vegetable is often at its best when it still has some "crunch" to it.

AUBERGINES

These are long, pear-shaped vegetables with a shiny, purple skin. They may be anything from 7.5 to 30cm long (3 to 12 inches). To par-cook aubergines, wipe the outside and cut the whole vegetable into bite-sized cubes, discarding the stalk end. If your aubergine is young and fresh, there is no need to remove the seeds. Steaming or microwaving is the best way to par-cook - boiled aubergines tend to absorb too much water and become soggy. Aubergine discolours rapidly once cut, so cook as quickly as possible. Whichever cooking method you use, 2-3 minutes should be enough.

BEANS

There is an enormous variety of beans available: runner beans, French beans and broad beans are the most common. Runner beans need to be topped and tailed, and the long edges thinly shaved to remove any strings, before being cut into 2.5cm (1 inch) long diagonal pieces. French beans need only be topped and tailed and straight cut into 2.5cm (1 inch) pieces. Broad beans should be removed from their pods. If they are old and a little tough, they should be skinned to reveal the green, inner beans. Blanch all kinds of beans in boiling water for three or four minutes.

BROCCOLI

Broccoli or calabrese is available in large heads. The stalk should be trimmed and cut into small florets. Sprouting broccoli, whether purple or white, comes in smaller heads. You will need to trim away some of the leaves. Blanch broccoli in boiling water for 2-3 minutes.

CARROTS

This familiar, bright orange vegetable should be topped and tailed, and, unless very young, peeled. A vegetable peeler makes this job easy. Carrots can be cut into rings, cubes or matchsticks and should be blanched in boiling water for 5 minutes.

CAULIFLOWER

This vegetable has a particular affinity with curry spices. Its creamy white head seems to capture the flavours of a Balti and will also pick up the colours of turmeric, paprika etc. Trim the stalk and cut the head into small florets before blanching it in boiling water for 2-3 minutes.

CELERY

White or green celery is available. Trim the leaves (which can be retained for an attractive garnish) and the base and cut across the stalks to give small, curved slices. These can be blanched in boiling water for 2-3 minutes, but raw celery gives a delicious crunch to a Balti.

COURGETTES

These popular vegetables are now available all year round and are most plentiful (and therefore cheaper) in late summer. Choose small, thin, firm courgettes about 2.5cm (1 inch) in diameter and 7.5-10cm (3-4 inches) long. These should be cut into 5mm (¼ inch) thick slices. They cook so quickly that they can usually be added to your Balti without blanching them. Courgettes do not need to be peeled but can sometimes taste a little bitter. If this is the case, steaming or microwaving them for a couple of minutes will help.

MUSHROOMS

Nowadays there is a wide range of mushrooms on supermarket or greengrocers' shelves. Button mushrooms are most often used for Baltis. Look out for chestnut mushrooms, too, which are slightly firmer in texture and have a brown cap. Mushrooms only need to be peeled if the skin is very tough. They can be sliced or diced, and baby button mushrooms can be used whole. There is no need for par-cooking, they can be popped into your Balti dish about 10 minutes before the end of the cooking time.

OKRA

This vegetable, looking like long, green, grooved spices, is also sold as bhindi or ladies' fingers. Okra no longer than 10cm (4 inches) is best. When you cut okra into rings, you will find that a sap starts to ooze. Don't make the mistake I made when first handling okra - I tried to wash off the sap and ended up with a colander full of slime. The more I washed, the more sap appeared. Instead, heat a tablespoon of oil in a pan and sizzle sliced or whole okra for a few minutes before adding to your Balti dish.

ONIONS

You'll be hard pressed to find a Balti recipe that doesn't include onions, for they add body and texture as well as flavour. There is no need to par-cook them - just peel and cut according to the recipe.

PARSNIPS

This is a vegetable that people tend either to love or to hate. It looks like a giant, knobbly white carrot and its flesh has a sweetish taste. Trim the top and bottom from the parsnip, peel quite thickly, and cut into small cubes or chips. Blanch in boiling water until just tender - about 8-10 minutes.

PEAS

The easiest way to use peas in your Balti dishes is to keep a bag of ready-frozen peas in the freezer and simply shake them into the Balti a few minutes before the end of cooking. If you are using fresh, shelled peas, however, blanch them in boiling water for 2-3 minutes first.

Mangetout is a variety of pea that is eaten in the pod while the peas are still tiny inside. It is an excellent vegetable for stir frying and adds a lovely splash of bright green to a Balti dish.

PEPPERS

These belong to the same family as chillies. Red and green peppers are common, but yellow, orange and purple ones are also increasingly available from supermarkets and greengrocers. They are particularly good for adding colour to a dish. To prepare a pepper, trim off the stalk end, cut in half lengthways and scrape out the seeds - unlike chillies, pepper seeds are not eaten. Peppers can be cut into strips or cubes, or if you are feeling artistic, into diamonds and other decorative shapes. They can be added, unblanched, towards the end of cooking a Balti, to add crunch and colour and, of course, a delicious flavour.

POTATOES

Surely the most versatile of vegetables, potatoes are wonderful in Balti dishes. They soak up the spicy sauce and become full of flavour. Old potatoes should be scrubbed, if the skin is left on, or peeled. Cut them into even-sized chunks and boil until just tender. Different varieties of potato require different cooking times and have individual characteristics. The best potato for a Balti will soften but not become floury or mushy when cooked. Maris Piper or Estima are good all-round potatoes. Baby new potatoes can be boiled until just tender, in their skins, and added whole.

Sweet potatoes are not relations, but their sweet, orange-yellow flesh makes an interesting addition to curries. Peel, dice and boil until just tender.

SPINACH

This is another vegetable that can be used successfully from the deep freeze. Simply thaw and drain it before adding to a Balti dish. If you can find fresh spinach (or grow your own), remove the thick stalks and sweat the leaves in a very little water until they wilt and reduce considerably in bulk. Drain well. Spinach combines with many dishes almost as a sauce, rather than remaining in distinct pieces.

SWEETCORN

You can strip the leaves and strings off cobs of corn, then scrape off the grains and cook in boiling water until tender. Or ... you can whip a bag of frozen sweetcorn kernels out of the freezer or open a can! Sweetcorn is a robust vegetable that survives freezing and canning admirably.

An attractive alternative in your Balti cooking is baby corn. The tiny cobs are readily available in supermarkets and taste deliciously sweet and tender. Add them whole, halved lengthways, or cut into slices about 10 minutes before the end of your Balti dish's cooking time.

TOMATOES

Usually available as round, red fruit, tomatoes may also be oval (plum tomatoes) or a golden yellow colour. They range in size from little cherry tomatoes to the huge beefsteak varieties. Tomatoes add a sharp sweetness to almost any Balti dish. Simply peel them (see Cook's tip on page 176) and chop them into fairly small pieces -they can then be added at any stage of cooking. Sweet and juicy cherry tomatoes can be added whole or halved and need not be peeled.

TURNIPS

These can be used as a useful substitute for some of the more exotic but hard to find vegetables used in traditional Baltis, such as tinda and lotus root. Prepare them as you would potatoes.

BABY VEGETABLES

In many supermarkets you will now find these tiny vegetables, minia- ture versions of familiar varieties. Courgettes, cauliflower, leeks and carrots are frequently available. They are more expensive than full-sized specimens but are very tender and look attractive in vegetable side dishes. Try to use them whole, as cutting them rather destroys their miniature perfection. They are usually packed to a very even size, so cutting should not be necessary.

LEGUMES

Lentils, dried peas, beans and pulses all fall into this category. Where once they were often thought of as a mainstay of vegetarian diets, legumes are now beginning to be appreciated as the highly nutritious and economical food they are. Because they can be stored for very long periods in their dry state, they once proved a valuable source of protein for the nomadic peoples of Baltistan during the hard winters.

Lentils add texture to Balti sauces and provide the basis for the well known Indian dish called dahl. Red or yellow lentils tend to lose their shape when cooked but have a floury quality that adds body to dishes. Other peas and beans keep their shape and provide an interesting, nutty texture in dishes, as well as making them hearty and substantial.

All legumes should be thoroughly washed before cooking as you may find some small stones amongst them. Soak the legumes in cold water before cooking - about 30 minutes for small lentils, 3-4 hours for larger lentils and split peas, and 12 hours or overnight for whole peas and beans. This makes the legumes slightly less starchy and softens them, so the cooking time is shorter.

Legumes should be boiled in a large saucepan. They will swell up to twice their dried size once cooked, so allow for this in your choice of pan. The following times are suggested as a guide for cooking legumes, but you will probably also find instructions on the packet.

Small lentils: simmer for about 30 minutes

Large lentils and split peas: simmer for 50-60 minutes

Chick peas: simmer for 1½ hours

Black eyed beans: simmer for 50-60 minutes

Kidney beans: boil briskly for 10 minutes (to kill toxins), then simmer for 60 minutes

If you wish, you can add some extra flavour by including 5ml (1tspn) of turmeric or Balti spice mix (see page 53) and a sliced onion in the cooking water.

In supermarkets legumes can be found in 500g (about 1lb) packs. It is most economical to cook the whole packet and then freeze what you don't need immediately in small cartons.

Canned legumes are usually packed in 400g (14oz) cans. Drain them well and rinse beans and peas before using them in a recipe, as there is often a starchy residue at the bottom of the can. Drained weight will be about 275-300g (10-11oz). This is the equivalent to the "cooked weight" of legumes you have cooked yourself.

♣ MIXED VEGETABLE BALTI ♣

This is quite a dry vegetable dish that would make an excellent accompaniment to a more saucy Balti. If you want to serve it as a main course, you might like to add about 150ml (¼pt) of Balti sauce (see page 56) to make a moister dish. You can choose which vegetables to include - potatoes, carrots, peas, green beans and cauliflower are particularly good.

PREPARATION TIME: 30 MINUTES

450g (1lb) mixed vegetables, cut into bite-sized pieces

30ml (2tbspn) ghee or vegetable oil

1 small onion, finely chopped

1 clove garlic, crushed

5ml (1tspn) chilli powder

10ml (2tspn) ground coriander

2.5ml (½tspn) turmeric

2 tomatoes, skinned and chopped

1 Heat the ghee or oil in a Balti pan, wok or large frying pan over a medium heat. Add the onion and garlic and cook until golden brown.

2 Add the chilli powder, coriander and turmeric and cook for 2-3 minutes, stirring all the time.

3 Add the vegetables, tomatoes and 45ml (3tbspn) of water. Cover the pan and simmer for 12-15 minutes, until the vegetables are tender, stirring occasionally.

4 If using, add the Balti sauce about 10 minutes before the end of the cooking time.

♣ DRY LENTIL BALTI ♣

This dish is best served as an accompaniment to a fairly light Balti, as lentils are quite filling. For a main meal, you may like to add more spice and onions.

PREPARATION TIME: 40 MINUTES + 30 MINUTES SOAKING TIME

225g (8oz) red lentils, soaked for 30 minutes in cold water

5ml (1tspn) turmeric

10ml (2tspn) Balti spice mix (see page 53)

225g (8oz) can chopped tomatoes

15ml (1tbspn) fresh coriander, chopped

1 small onion, chopped

1 green chilli, finely chopped

30ml (2tbspn) ghee or vegetable oil

1 Drain the lentils and place in a saucepan with 425ml (¾pt) of cold water, the turmeric and the Balti spice mix. Bring to the boil and simmer for 20 minutes, or until tender. Mash the lentils lightly with a fork.

2 Stir in the tomatoes and coriander. Simmer for a further 20 minutes.

3 Meanwhile, heat the ghee or oil in a pan over a medium to high heat. Add the onion and chilli and fry for about 5 minutes until golden brown.

4 Turn the lentil mix into a serving dish and top with the onion mixture.

✤ POTATO BALTI ✤

Potatoes soak up the flavour of herbs and spices beautifully. Serve with a mixed vegetable curry for a vegetarian meal, or as a side dish with a fairly light meat Balti.

PREPARATION TIME: 35 MINUTES

450g (1lb) potatoes, diced and par-cooked

1 onion

45ml (3tbspn) ghee or vegetable oil

5ml (1tspn) chilli powder

2.5ml (½tspn) turmeric

2.5cm (1 inch) cube fresh root ginger, grated

Pinch of salt

5ml (1tspn) Balti garam masala (see page 54)

15ml (1tbspn) fresh coriander, finely chopped

1 Grate the onion coarsely. This should give a watery pulp.

2 Heat the ghee or oil in a Balti pan, wok or large frying pan over a medium heat and add the onion. Fry for about 5-10 minutes, until golden.

3 Add the chilli powder, turmeric and ginger and fry for 2-3 minutes, stirring. Stir in 150ml (¼pt) of water.

4 Add the potatoes and salt and simmer gently for about 20-25 minutes, until the sauce has thickened and the potatoes are fully cooked.

5 Serve, sprinkled with garam masala and coriander.

✤ OKRA BALTI ✤

If you have not handled okra before, be sure to read the notes at the beginning of this chapter, but don't be put off! It is a delicious vegetable.

PREPARATION TIME: 30 MINUTES

450g (1lb) okra, cut into 1cm (½ inch) lengths

45ml (3tspn) ghee or vegetable oil

1 onion, chopped

15ml (1tbspn) Balti spice mix (see page 53)

225g (8oz) potatoes, cut into 1cm (½ inch) cubes

Salt

1 Heat the ghee or oil in a Balti pan, wok or frying pan over a medium heat. Add the onion and cook until tender and just colouring - about 10 minutes.

2 Add the Balti spice mix and cook for 2 minutes, stirring all the time.

3 Add the potato pieces and fry for 2-3 minutes, then add the okra. Cover and cook for 10-12 minutes, or until the potatoes are tender. Add salt to taste. If the mix becomes too dry during cooking, add a further 15ml (1tbspn) of ghee or vegetable oil or a little water.

♣ SPICY SWEETCORN BALTI ♣

Sweetcorn is excellent in a vegetable Balti as it adds a splash of colour as well as flavour. In this recipe you can use blanched fresh, canned or frozen sweetcorn.

PREPARATION TIME: 30 MINUTES

45ml (3tbspn) ghee or vegetable oil

1 small onion, finely chopped

1 medium potato, cut into 1cm (½ inch) cubes

225g (8oz) sweetcorn

10ml (2tspn) Balti spice mix (see page 53)

1 small green pepper, seeded and cut into strips

225g (8oz) can chopped tomatoes

Salt

15ml (1tbspn) fresh coriander, chopped

5ml (1tspn) Balti garam masala (see page 54)

1 Heat the ghee or oil in a Balti pan, wok or frying pan over a medium heat. Add the onion and cook for about 10 minutes or until tender and just beginning to colour.

2 Add the potatoes and stir fry for 5 minutes.

3 Add the sweetcorn and spice mix and cook for 5 minutes, stirring all the time.

4 Add the pepper and tomatoes, cover and simmer for 7-10 minutes or until the potatoes are tender. Add salt to taste.

5 Stir in the coriander and garam masala and serve.

❧ SPICY AUBERGINE BALTI ❧

This dish has a rich sauce, good with a dry, mince-based Balti and lots of chappatis. Courgettes would work well in this dish instead of the aubergines.

PREPARATION TIME: 25 MINUTES

450g (1lb) aubergine, cut into 2.5cm (1 inch) cubes

45ml (3tbspn) ghee or vegetable oil

1 large onion, chopped

2 cloves garlic, crushed

2 green chillies, finely chopped

275ml (½pt) Balti sauce (see page 56)

15ml (1tbspn) fresh coriander, chopped

1 Heat the ghee or oil in a Balti pan, wok or large frying pan over a medium heat. Add the onion and garlic and cook for 8-10 minutes.

2 Add the chillies and cook for 2-3 minutes, then add the aubergine chunks.

3 Add the Balti sauce, cover and simmer gently for about 10 minutes, stirring occasionally. (Stir gently towards the end of the cooking time, or the aubergine may disintegrate.)

4 Stir in the coriander and serve.

♣ CHICK PEA AND MUSHROOM BALTI ♣

Chick peas make an excellent basis for vegetarian Balti meals but need some strong flavours with them to overcome their natural blandness.

PREPARATION TIME: 20 MINUTES

400g (14oz) can chick peas, drained and rinsed or

275g (10oz) dried chick peas, cooked (see page 147)

225g (8oz) button mushrooms, sliced

60ml (4tbspn) ghee or vegetable oil

2 onions, chopped

1 green chilli, chopped

4 tomatoes, skinned and chopped

10ml (2tspn) Balti spice mix (see page 53)

15ml (1tbspn) fresh coriander, chopped

Salt

1 Heat the ghee or oil in a Balti pan, wok or frying pan over a medium heat. Add the onions and fry for about 10 minutes, until they are just beginning to colour.

2 Add the chilli and tomatoes and cook for 2 minutes.

3 Add the chick peas and spice mix with 150ml (¼pt) of water and simmer for 5 minutes.

4 Add the mushrooms and coriander and stir fry for a further 3-4 minutes. Add salt to taste and serve.

✤ KIDNEY BEAN BALTI ✤

Red kidney beans have a delicious, nutty taste and texture and a wonderful colour. If cooking your own kidney beans, you must boil them hard for the first ten minutes of cooking time to kill off the toxins in the beans. They are perfectly safe once you have done this. If you are using canned beans, of course, this has already been done for you.

PREPARATION TIME: 30 MINUTES

225g (8oz) dried red kidney beans, soaked overnight and cooked (see page 148)

or 400g (14oz) can red kidney beans, drained and rinsed

45ml (3 tbspn) ghee or vegetable oil

1 clove garlic, crushed

1 green chilli, chopped

3 tomatoes, skinned and chopped

10ml (2tspn) Balti spice mix (see page 53)

150ml (¼pt) Balti sauce (see page 56)

2.5ml (½tspn) dried fenugreek

15ml (1tbspn) fresh coriander, chopped

1 Heat the ghee or oil in a Balti pan, wok or frying pan over a medium heat. Add the garlic and chilli and cook for 2-3 minutes.

2 Add the tomatoes and spice mix and cook for 5 minutes, stirring all the time.

3 Stir in the Balti sauce and fenugreek and add the kidney beans. Reduce the heat and simmer for about 20 minutes, adding more sauce if it seems too dry.

4 Stir in the coriander and serve.

♣ MUSHROOM AND PEA BALTI ♣

You will find mushrooms in many Balti vegetable dishes. They seem to absorb the spice flavours particularly well. Peas add a touch of brightness - be careful not to overcook them or they will lose their colour.

PREPARATION TIME: 30 MINUTES

350g (12oz) button mushrooms

225g (8oz) peas

45ml (3tbspn) ghee or vegetable oil

2.5 ml (½tspn) turmeric

2.5ml (½tspn) ground cumin

2.5ml (½tspn) chilli powder

275ml (½pt) Balti sauce (see page 56)

2.5ml (½tspn) dried fenugreek

5ml (1tspn) Balti garam masala (see page 54)

15ml (1tbspn) fresh coriander, chopped

1 Wash, drain and thickly slice the mushrooms, cutting in half if very large. Defrost the peas if frozen.

2 Heat the ghee or oil in a Balti pan, wok or frying pan over a medium heat. Add the peas and spices and cook for 5 minutes.

3 Stir in the Balti sauce and simmer, stirring occasionally, for about 15 minutes.

4 Add the fenugreek and garam masala and cook for a further 5 minutes.

5 Stir in the coriander and serve.

♣ BLACK EYED BEAN, SPINACH ♣ AND MUSHROOM BALTI

This slightly more complex vegetable dish would make an excellent main course for a vegetarian Balti meal. The black eyed beans have a slightly sweet and nutty taste, which combines particularly well with mushrooms. The spinach adds a richness to the whole dish.

PREPARATION TIME: 15 MINUTES

400g (14oz) can black eyed beans, drained and rinsed

200g (7oz) frozen spinach, thawed and drained

110g (4oz) button mushrooms, sliced

45ml (3tbspn) ghee or vegetable oil

2.5cm (1 inch) cube fresh root ginger, grated

2 cloves garlic, crushed

1 green chilli, chopped finely

30ml (2tbspn) Balti spice mix (page 53)

15ml (1tbspn) fresh coriander, chopped

3 tomatoes, peeled and chopped

150ml (¼pt) Balti sauce (see page 56)

Salt

1 Heat the ghee or oil in a Balti pan, wok or large frying pan over a medium heat. Add the ginger, garlic and chilli and sizzle for 2 minutes.

2 Mix in the spinach, prodding it well with a wooden spoon to break it up and blend it with the other ingredients.

3 Add the mushrooms and cook for 2-3 minutes.

4 Stir in the spice mix, coriander, tomatoes, black eyed beans and Balti sauce. Bring to the boil, stirring, and simmer for about 5 minutes. If the mix appears dry, add a little more sauce.

5 Add salt to taste and serve.

Cook's tip

If you are cooking your own beans, you will need half the weight of dry beans to the weight of can suggested in the recipe. This is a useful rough guide for all legumes. If you have cooked a batch of beans and frozen them, use about three-quarters of the can weight, remembering that part of the can weight is made up of the liquid in which the beans are packed.

If you are lucky enough to have fresh spinach, start off with twice the amount of frozen spinach in the recipe. Cook, drain and chop quite finely before using.

♣ SWEETCORN AND POTATO BALTI ♣

This is one of my favourite Balti dishes - I could happily finish an entire batch before it ever reached the table! The potatoes pick up the flavours of the spices beautifully and the sweetcorn makes this a very attractive dish. In this recipe, the slightly softer texture of canned sweetcorn works better than frozen or fresh.

PREPARATION TIME: 30 MINUTES

400g (14oz) can sweetcorn, drained

2 large potatoes

45ml (3tbspn) ghee or vegetable oil

2.5ml (1 inch) cube fresh ginger, grated

2 cloves garlic, crushed

1 green chilli, finely chopped

150ml (¼pt) Balti sauce (see page 56)

15ml (1tbspn) tomato purée

10ml (2tspn) Balti garam masala (see page 54)

15ml (1tbspn) fresh coriander, chopped

Salt

1 Cut the potatoes into even-sized pieces and boil in lightly salted water until just (but only just) tender. Drain and allow to cool slightly before cutting into bite-sized cubes.

2 Heat the ghee or oil in a Balti pan, wok or frying pan over a medium heat. Add the potato pieces, ginger, garlic and chilli. Cook, stirring, for about 5 minutes.

3 Add the sweetcorn, Balti sauce and tomato purée and mix well. Simmer gently for 8-10 minutes, until the potatoes are cooked. Stir

gently so that the potatoes retain their cube shape. Add a little more sauce if necessary.

4 Stir in the garam masala, coriander and salt to taste. Serve.

✤ BALTI CARROTS, PEAS AND ✤ POTATOES

Here is a simple and colourful dish that is very quick to make, particularly if you have some leftover cold boiled potatoes in the fridge. Although excellent as a side dish with a Balti main course, this recipe is also very good served with grilled sausages or chops.

PREPARATION TIME: 25 MINUTES + PAR-COOKING TIME FOR POTATOES

175g (6oz) carrots, peeled and cut into 1cm (½ inch) cubes

175g (6oz) peas, fresh or frozen (defrosted)

2 large potatoes, par-cooked (see page 144)

30ml (2tbspn) ghee or vegetable oil

175g (6oz) onions, chopped

10ml (2tspn) Balti spice mix (see page 53)

Salt

1 Heat the ghee or oil in a Balti pan, wok or large frying pan over a medium heat. Add the onion and cook for about 10 minutes or until tender and just starting to brown.

2 Add the spice mix, carrots, peas and a little water. Stir fry for about 10 minutes until the vegetables are tender. Add a little more water if necessary, to stop the mixture sticking, but remember that this is meant to be quite a dry dish.

3 Add the potatoes and heat for 2-3 minutes. Add salt to taste and serve.

✤ SPICY GREEN BEAN BALTI ✤

This dish makes an excellent accompaniment to almost any meat or fish dish. It is quite hot, so you may like to be slightly more cautious with the chillies than suggested here.

PREPARATION TIME: 20 MINUTES

450g (1lb) French beans, topped and tailed

30ml (2tbspn) ghee or vegetable oil

2.5cm (1 inch) cube fresh root ginger, grated

3 cloves garlic, crushed

2 red chillies, chopped

2.5ml (½tspn) ground cumin

2.5ml (½tspn) ground coriander

150ml (¼pt) Balti sauce (see page 56)

Salt

Juice of half a lemon

Pinch of Balti garam masala (see page 54)

1 Cut the beans across to give 5mm (¼ inch) pieces. You can cut up a bunch in one go with the aid of a large, sharp cook's knife.

2 Heat the ghee or oil in a Balti pan, wok or frying pan over a medium heat. Add the ginger and garlic and cook for 5 minutes.

3 Add the chillies and spices and cook for a further 2 minutes, stirring.

4 Add the Balti sauce and beans and simmer for about 10 minutes, until the beans are tender.

5 Add salt to taste. Just before serving, squeeze over the lemon juice and sprinkle with garam masala.

♣ MUSHROOM AND RED PEPPER ♣ BALTI

This must be one of the quickest Balti recipes in existence. It makes a delicious snack simply served with some naan bread, or is a tasty and colourful side dish.

PREPARATION TIME: 15 MINUTES

450g (1lb) button mushrooms

1 large red pepper, deseeded and cut into 1cm (½ inch) dice

30ml (2tbspn) ghee or vegetable oil

110g (4oz) onions, coarsely chopped

2.5ml (½tspn) cumin seeds

15ml (1tbspn) Balti spice mix (see page 53)

Salt

1 Heat the ghee or oil in a Balti pan, wok or frying pan over a medium to high heat. Add the onions and cook for about 8 minutes until tender and golden brown.

2 Add the cumin seeds and spice mix and cook for 2 minutes.

3 Add the mushrooms, cut into quarters if over 1cm (½ inch) in diameter, and the red pepper. Briskly stir fry for 5 minutes.

4 Add salt to taste and serve.

ACCOMPANIMENTS

RECIPES

1 CHAPPATIS

Wholewheat unleavened breads

2 PARATHAS

Dough layered with ghee or unsalted butter to give a puffy texture

3 NAAN BREAD

A soft bread made with yeast (and a quicker, unleavened version)

4 PURIS

Deep-fried bread

5 TOMATO AND ONION SALAD

6 ONION AND CUCUMBER RAITA

A cooling accompaniment to a spicy Balti

7 FRESH CORIANDER CHUTNEY

8 SPICY FRUITED CHUTNEY

9 APPLE AND APRICOT CHUTNEY

10 CRISPY ONIONS

A crunchy garnish or nibble

As already stated, Balti dishes are basically complete meals in a pan and therefore do not require the many accompaniments and side dishes usually served with traditional curries.

The one essential accompaniment, however, is bread. There is quite a variety to choose from. I have tended to concentrate on the plainer breads – so as not to detract from the flavour of the Balti – but of course you can be more adventurous, adding coriander or cumin seeds and perhaps chopped, fresh coriander, onions or garlic.

Suit your bread to your curry. A light curry may require a more substantial bread, such as naan, while a more robust Balti is best served with a less filling bread, such as chappatis or puris.

While your guests wait for their Balti, it is always nice to serve a few poppadoms – the Indian equivalent of peanuts or crisps. These are even tastier with a selection of homemade chutneys and dips. There are hundreds of recipes for these, that would fill a whole book by themselves, so I have included just a few favourites to start you off.

♣ CHAPPATIS ♣

These are flat, round breads, cooked in a dry pan and then grilled. The dough must be rested for at least 30 minutes before using and can be kept, wrapped in cling film, for up to a week in the refrigerator. Chappatis are simple breads but do require practice to make perfectly. Don't worry if your early efforts look a bit misshapen – they will still taste good!

MAKES: 12-14 CHAPPATIS

PREPARATION TIME: 30-40 MINUTES + AT LEAST 30 MINUTES RESTING TIME

225g (8oz) wholemeal flour

110g (4oz) plain white flour

2.5ml (½tspn) salt

About 175ml (6 fl oz) warm water

Ghee or unsalted butter, melted

1 Sift the flours into a bowl with the salt. Add enough water, a little at a time, to form a soft dough.

2 Knead the dough until it becomes less sticky - about 10 minutes. Wrap in cling film and leave to rest for at least 30 minutes.

3 Divide the dough into 12-14 evenly sized pieces and shape into balls. On a floured surface, roll each ball into a circle about 15cm (6 inches) in diameter.

4 Preheat the grill to high. Heat a frying pan over a medium heat and place a chappati into it. Cook one side until brown spots appear. After a little while you will instinctively know when the chappati needs turning, but for the first few times, you will need to keep

peering underneath using a palette knife or fish slice to help you. If the chappati burns, quickly reduce the heat; if it sticks, increase the heat slightly. When the first side is cooked, turn the chappati and cook the other side.

5 Remove the chappati from the pan and place under the hot grill. After a few seconds, the chappati will puff up. Repeat with the other side.

6 Brush the finished chappati with a little melted butter or ghee and keep warm while cooking the others.

Chappatis are at their best eaten at once, but they can be successfully reheated, either in a microwave, or, wrapped in foil, in the oven. They also freeze well, for up to a month, and can be defrosted and reheated as above.

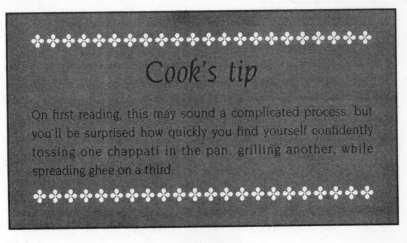

Cook's tip

On first reading, this may sound a complicated process, but you'll be surprised how quickly you find yourself confidently tossing one chappati in the pan, grilling another, while spreading ghee on a third.

♣ PARATHAS ♣

These are made with a similar dough to chappatis, but they are layered with ghee, cooked first in a dry pan, and then again brushed with a little ghee.

MAKES: 14-16 PARATHAS

PREPARATION TIME: ABOUT 30 MINUTES

350g (12oz) plain flour

2.5ml (½tspn) salt

60ml (4tbspn) vegetable oil

About 175ml (6 fl oz) warm water

Melted ghee or unsalted butter

1 Sift the flour into a bowl and add the salt. Mix the water and oil and add to the flour slowly. Mix to a sticky dough.

2 Knead the dough for about 10 minutes, until no longer sticky, and divide into 14-16 pieces.

3 Roll the pieces into balls and flatten, on a floured surface, to 20cm (8 inch) circles. Brush with melted ghee, fold into semicircles, brush with more ghee, and fold in half again to make a small triangle. With a rolling pin, gently roll these triangles until they are quite thin.

4 Heat a frying pan over a medium heat and place a triangle in it. Cook for about 1 minute, until brown specks appear on the underside. Turn and cook the other side in the same way, but while it is cooking, brush the cooked surface with melted ghee. Turn again and brush the newly cooked surface with melted ghee while cooking for 30 seconds. Turn again and cook for a further 30 seconds. This way, each side should be cooked dry for 1 minute and with ghee for 30 seconds.

5 Wrap the cooked parathas in foil to keep warm while cooking the rest. These are best eaten immediately, but can also be successfully reheated, wrapped in foil, in the oven.

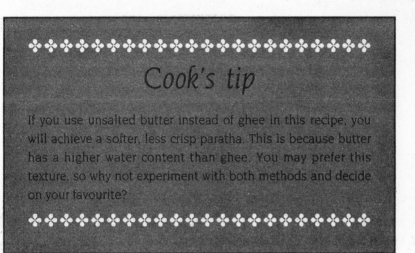

Cook's tip

If you use unsalted butter instead of ghee in this recipe, you will achieve a softer, less crisp paratha. This is because butter has a higher water content than ghee. You may prefer this texture, so why not experiment with both methods and decide on your favourite?

♣ NAAN BREAD ♣

Naan bread is traditionally cooked by slapping the uncooked dough on the sides of a tandoor - a clay oven in which tandoori foods are cooked. The dough sags slightly as it cooks and this results in the teardrop-shaped bread we are used to seeing. Assuming you don't have a tandoor lurking in the corner of your kitchen, use your domestic oven, turned up to maximum. Personally, I simply shape the bread into rounds, but you can copy the traditional shape if you wish.

I have included two recipes for naan. The quick recipe doesn't use yeast and therefore doesn't need proving time. It produces a deliciously light bread, but needs to be eaten at once. The yeast recipe takes longer, but results in a bread suitable for freezing and reheating. Instructions for cooking both kinds of naan follow the recipes.

QUICK NAAN BREAD

MAKES: 6 NAAN

PREPARATION TIME: 30 MINUTES

450g (1lb) self-raising flour

5ml (1tspn) salt

2.5ml (½tspn) baking powder

30ml (2tbspn) melted ghee or vegetable oil

60ml (4tbspn) natural yoghurt

2 eggs, beaten

150ml (¼pt) cold water

1 Sift the flour, salt and baking powder into a bowl. Add the melted ghee or oil, the yoghurt and eggs, and mix together lightly.

2 Add the water, a little at a time, to produce a soft dough. Use your hands to bring the dough together, or whiz the whole mixture in a food processor, in which case slightly less water will be required.

3 Knead the dough for 2-3 minutes, until it is smooth.

YEASTED NAAN BREAD

Makes: 6 naan

Preparation time: About 1½ hours

150ml (¼pt) hand-hot milk

5ml (1tspn) sugar

25g (1oz) fresh yeast

450g (1lb) plain flour

5ml (1tspn) salt

30ml (2tbspn) melted ghee or vegetable oil

150ml (¼pt) natural yoghurt

1 egg, beaten

1 Cream together the yeast and sugar until liquid and stir into the milk. Leave in a warm place until a froth forms on the top.

2 Sift the flour and salt into a bowl. Make a well in the centre, add the remaining ingredients and mix to a dough. Knead for about 5 minutes, until the dough is smooth and elastic, then place it in a large, floured bowl. Cover with a clean tea towel and leave in a warm place for about an hour, until the dough has doubled in size.

3 Knead again for about 5 minutes, to knock out the air.

COOKING NAAN

1 Preheat your oven to its highest setting and heat a baking tray in it. At the same time, heat the grill.

2 Divide the dough, whether quick or yeasted, into 6 pieces and shape into rounds.

3 Carefully remove the baking tray from the oven, quickly slap a naan on to it, and return to the oven for 3-4 minutes.

4 Remove the tray from the oven and place under a hot grill for a minute to crisp and brown the top. You can, of course, cook two naan at once if the sizes of your baking tray and grill permit.

5 Keep the naan warm, wrapped in a clean tea towel, or cool for freezing and reheating.

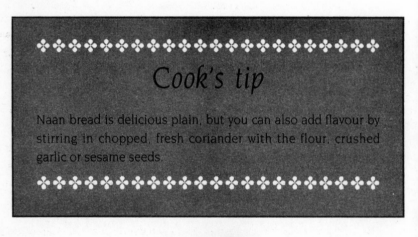

Cook's tip

Naan bread is delicious plain, but you can also add flavour by stirring in chopped, fresh coriander with the flour, crushed garlic or sesame seeds.

♣ PURIS ♣

Unlike the other breads in this section, puris are fried, which gives them quite a different flavour to chappatis. They need to be eaten very soon after making and should not be reheated or frozen.

MAKES: 25 PURIS

PREPARATION TIME: 50-60 MINUTES

350g (12oz) plain white flour

110g (4oz) wholemeal flour

30ml (2tbspn) vegetable oil (plus extra for deep frying)

200ml (7 fl oz) cold water

1 Sieve the flour into a bowl and add the cooking oil. Mix and slowly add water until a slightly soft dough is achieved. Knead gently for a few minutes and divide into 25 pieces.

2 Roll out each piece, on a floured surface, to give a circle about 12cm (5 inches) across.

3 Heat the oil in a deep frying pan, Balti pan or wok. Once hot, keep at a steady temperature over a medium heat. Place a puri in the oil and fry for about 20 seconds. Quickly turn and cook on the other side for about the same time. The puri should puff up and turn golden brown.

4 Drain the puri on kitchen paper and keep warm in a low oven until all the puris are fried. Then serve at once.

♣ TOMATO AND ONION SALAD ♣

This provides a delicious dip for poppadoms. It is particularly good if served straight from the refrigerator.

SERVES: 4–6

PREPARATION TIME: 10 MINUTES

1 large onion, finely chopped

2 firm tomatoes, peeled and finely chopped

2 green chillies, finely chopped

A few sprigs of coriander and/or mint

Juice of a lemon

Pinch of salt

Pinch of sugar

Mix all the ingredients together, ensuring that the sugar has dissolved. Cover and leave in the refrigerator until ready to serve.

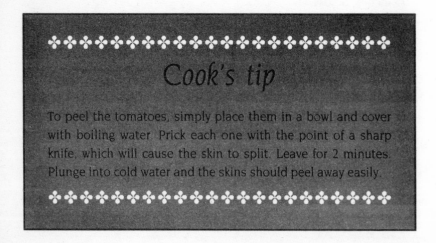

Cook's tip

To peel the tomatoes, simply place them in a bowl and cover with boiling water. Prick each one with the point of a sharp knife, which will cause the skin to split. Leave for 2 minutes. Plunge into cold water and the skins should peel away easily.

❖ ONION AND CUCUMBER RAITA ❖

This easily prepared dip is especially good with spicy poppadoms as it cools down the heat beautifully.

SERVES: 4-6

PREPARATION TIME: 15 MINUTES

425ml (³⁄₄pt) natural yoghurt

110g (4oz) cucumber

1 large onion

2.5ml (½tspn) cumin seeds

Pinch of salt

Pinch of chilli powder

A little freshly ground black pepper

A little chopped fresh coriander

1 Peel the cucumber and cut it into small cubes, about 1cm (½ inch) square.

2 Finely chop the onion.

3 Mix together the yoghurt, cucumber, onion, cumin seeds, salt, chilli powder and pepper and turn into a serving dish. Cover and chill well.

4 Just before serving, sprinkle with the coriander.

♣ FRESH CORIANDER CHUTNEY ♣

In Indian cookery there are two types of chutney: cooked and uncooked. The cooked ones, such as mango chutney, are similar to the chutneys that we often serve with cold meats or cheese, and store well. The uncooked type, of which this recipe is an example, should be made and eaten as freshly as possible, although they should keep in a refrigerator for a few days. Coriander chutney has a very refreshing flavour and makes an excellent dip. It is best made in a liquidiser or food processor.

SERVES: 4-6

PREPARATION TIME: 15 MINUTES

110g (4oz) fresh coriander, weighed after trimming off the roots
and lower stems
1 green chilli
Juice of half a lemon
10g (½oz) fresh ginger
2.5ml (½tspn) salt
Freshly ground black pepper

1 Roughly chop the coriander and chilli. Grate the ginger finely.

2 Place all the ingredients in a liquidiser or food processor and work until a paste is achieved. You may have to scrape down the sides several times during the processing.

3 Turn into a non-metallic dish to serve.

♣ SPICY FRUITED CHUTNEY ♣

Cooked chutneys store well for at least a year. In fact, they are best stored for at least 6-8 weeks before you sample them, to allow time for the flavours to mingle and mellow. If you enjoy making chutneys, why not make extra and give them as presents to curry-loving friends - a circle of pretty paper placed over the lid and tied with ribbon turns a jam jar into a gift. This chutney is a good one to make after Christmas, with those leftover packets of dates and figs.

MAKES: ABOUT 3KG (6½LB)

PREPARATION TIME: ABOUT 4 HOURS

450g (1lb) cooking apples, weighed after peeling and coring

450g (1lb) tomatoes, skinned (see page 176)

225g (8oz) dried figs

225g (8oz) dates

225g (8oz) sultanas

225g (8oz) onions, peeled

10 green chillies

1.25 litres (2pt) malt vinegar

50g (2oz) salt

700g (1½lb) soft dark brown sugar

25g (1oz) fresh ginger, peeled and grated

1 Finely chop the apples, tomatoes, figs, dates, onions and chillies, and place in a preserving pan with the sultanas and 570ml (1pt) of the vinegar. Cover the pan (foil works perfectly well if you don't have a lid) and simmer until the pieces are tender - about 20 minutes.

2 Remove the lid and add the remaining vinegar, salt, sugar and the ginger. Stir thoroughly, bring to a very gentle simmer and cook for about 3 hours, stirring occasionally to ensure the mix doesn't stick to the bottom of the pan. By the end of this time, the chutney should be fairly smooth, with no excess liquid. To test for this, drag your wooden spoon across the surface of the chutney to make a sort of channel. The chutney is cooked if the channel doesn't immediately fill with liquid.

3 Carefully pour the chutney into hot, sterilised jars and allow to cool completely. Seal and label when cold.

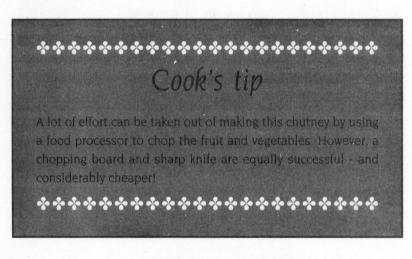

Cook's tip

A lot of effort can be taken out of making this chutney by using a food processor to chop the fruit and vegetables. However, a chopping board and sharp knife are equally successful - and considerably cheaper!

♣ APPLE AND APRICOT CHUTNEY ♣

This is a delicious fruity chutney, which successfully combines sweet, sour and hot flavours, but is still refreshing. It goes well with all Indian and Balti meals and has the added bonus of being an ideal accompaniment to roast gammon, pork chops, sausages and cold meats, especially ham.

MAKES: 1KG (2LBS)

PREPARATION TIME: ABOUT 1 HOUR

450g (1lb) cooking apples, weighed after peeling and coring

225g (8oz) dried apricots (no-need-to-soak type)

50g (2oz) sultanas

5 cloves of garlic, peeled

25g (1oz) fresh ginger, grated

425ml (¾pt) malt vinegar

420g (15oz) granulated sugar

10ml (2tspn) salt

5-10ml (1-2tspn) cayenne pepper (to taste)

1 Roughly chop the apples and apricots. Finely chop the garlic.

2 Mix all the ingredients in a preserving pan and cook over a medium heat for about 30 minutes, at quite a fast simmer, until a jam-like, pulpy texture is achieved. Stir fairly often towards the end of cooking, as the thicker the mixture becomes, the more likely it is to stick to the bottom of the pan.

3 Pour the mixture into warmed, sterilised jars and allow to cool completely. When cold, lid and label.

♣ CRISPY ONIONS ♣

This is a useful standby. It perks up any dish and adds flavour, texture and garnish with one quick sprinkle. Unfortunately, crispy onions also serve as a delicious nibble - store in a tightly closed air-tight jar and try to forget where they are!

MAKES: ABOUT 225G (8OZ)

PREPARATION TIME: ABOUT 30 MINUTES

225g (8oz) onions, peeled

Vegetable oil

1 Cut the onions in half from root to tip. Lay each half, cut side down, on a chopping board and cut across in the thinnest slices possible.

2 Heat about 1cm (½ inch) of oil in a large frying pan over a medium heat. When hot, add the onions and fry, stirring all the time, until they turn brown. Remove from the pan and spread out on kitchen paper. As they cool, they should become crisp.

3 When completely cold, pack the crispy onions into a screw-top jar and seal tightly. They will keep for 4 or 5 days.

Cook's tip

When slicing onions, a really sharp knife is called for. Pivot the point on your chopping board and bring the blade down so as literally to shave off a slice of onion.

DESSERTS

RECIPES

1 KULFI

Almond and pistachio ice-cream

2 VERMICELLI PUDDING

A dryish milk pudding

3 GULAB JAMAM

Little sponge cakes in syrup

4 CARROT HALVA

A sweet, grated carrot dessert

5 KHEER

An exotic version of rice pudding

6 SEMOLINA AND ALMOND HALVA

A sweet, fudgy cake

7 BARFI

Indian fudge

8 TROPICAL FRUIT SALAD

An Indian version of a classic dessert

9 MANGOES

D esserts from the Indian sub-continent tend to be very sweet and are often based on milk and nuts. On the whole they are not designed with weight-watchers in mind, but it should be remembered that because of their sweetness only very small portions are needed. Surprisingly, a very sweet dessert provides a wonderful antidote to a hot curry. All that is required is a small, strong coffee to round off a wonderful meal.

Alternatives to the more traditional Indian puddings are fresh fruit or fruit salad. Gone are the days when the only mango available in the United Kingdom was a canned yellow mush. Not only have canning techniques considerably improved, with fruit being poached in juice to retain its natural flavour, but supermarket shelves are now brimming with all kinds of exotic fresh fruits. Mangoes, lychees and guavas are probably the most traditional, but these combine wonderfully with pineapples, pawpaws and bananas.

Remember too that several of the desserts are very like sweets and would provide an intriguing alternative to mints at the end of a special dinner party.

♣ KULFI ♣

This popular Indian dessert is often served at weddings and other big celebrations, and is a particular favourite with children. It is time consuming but simple to prepare. When boiling the milk, arm yourself with a good but not too engrossing book!

SERVES: 6-8

PREPARATION TIME: ABOUT 90 MINUTES

2 litres (3½pt) full cream milk

10 whole cardamom pods

110g (4oz) granulated sugar

50g (2oz) chopped blanched almonds

25g (1oz) chopped unsalted pistachios

150ml (¼pt) single cream

1 Place the milk in a large, heavy based saucepan - a stock pan is ideal - and bring to the boil. Just as the milk begins to rise, turn down the heat to a level that keeps the milk at a vigorous simmer, without allowing it to boil over. Add the cardamom pods. The milk has to reduce to about one third of its original amount (see the Cook's tip opposite), that is, to about 700ml (1¼pt). Stir the milk often, mixing in the skin as it forms.

2 Once the milk is reduced, remove the cardamom pods and stir in the sugar and almonds. Simmer for 2-3 minutes, stirring all the while, until the sugar has dissolved. Remove from the heat. Pour into a howl and allow to cool completely. Stir in all of the cream and half of the pistachios.

3 If you have an ice-cream maker, you can now proceed according to

manufacturer's instructions. If not, turn the mixture into a shallow plastic container and place it in the freezer at its coldest setting. Stir the mixture every 30 minutes. Once it is becoming almost impossible to stir, you have two options:

a) Leave the mixture to freeze solid. Place it in the main body of the refrigerator half an hour before serving. Serve cut into small squares.

b) Traditionally kulfi is pressed into small conical moulds, frozen completely and turned out on to serving plates. Yoghurt pots make good substitutes for the moulds. Press the kulfi into the pots and freeze until firm. Turn out on to plates to serve.

Either way, just before serving, sprinkle the kulfi with the remaining chopped pistachios.

Cook's tip

Reducing a liquid to a third of its original amount need not involve a lot of messy transferring to and from measuring jugs. Before putting the pan of liquid on the heat, mark on the outside of the pan, with a marker pen, the level of the liquid inside. Now make another mark a third of the way between the base of the pan and the first mark - by eye is good enough, major mathematical calculations are not required. Now boil away and when you believe you are getting close to the desired reduction, remove the pan from the heat. Allow the liquid to subside and judge its position against your mark. Boil again if necessary.

♣ VERMICELLI PUDDING ♣

In India and Pakistan a very fine vermicelli is used. This is only available here at specialist stores, but a reasonably fine vermicelli should
be available in the pasta section of most supermarkets. This dessert is
not often found on restaurant menus, so is a special treat.

SERVES: 4

PREPARATION TIME: 45 MINUTES

50g (2oz) unsalted butter or ghee

175g (6oz) vermicelli, broken into about 5cm (2 inch) lengths

570ml (1pt) full fat milk, heated

2.5ml (½tspn) ground cardamom

2.5ml (½tspn) grated nutmeg

25g (1oz) chopped almonds

50g (2oz) sultanas (optional)

75g (3oz) sugar (or to taste)

1 Melt the butter or ghee in a heavy based saucepan over a low to
medium heat. Add the pieces of vermicelli and stir continuously until
the vermicelli turns golden brown. This may take 15-20 minutes, but
don't be tempted to turn up the heat. Watch carefully, as the colour
change can happen quite suddenly, and don't worry if some pieces
are darker than others.

2 Slowly stir in the milk. Heating it first reduces the risk of spitting.
Allow the milk to simmer without boiling over and add the spices,
nuts and sultanas (if using). Simmer fairly vigorously for about 20
minutes, stirring frequently, until much of the liquid has been
absorbed.

3 Add the sugar and simmer, still stirring, for a further 5 minutes. Transfer to a large bowl or individual dishes and serve hot or warm.

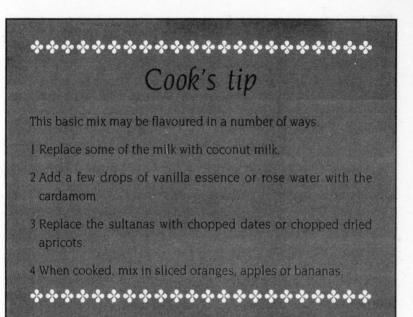

✤✤✤✤✤✤✤✤✤✤✤✤✤✤✤✤✤✤✤✤✤✤✤✤✤✤✤✤✤✤✤

Cook's tip

This basic mix may be flavoured in a number of ways.

1 Replace some of the milk with coconut milk.

2 Add a few drops of vanilla essence or rose water with the cardamom.

3 Replace the sultanas with chopped dates or chopped dried apricots.

4 When cooked, mix in sliced oranges, apples or bananas.

✤✤✤✤✤✤✤✤✤✤✤✤✤✤✤✤✤✤✤✤✤✤✤✤✤✤✤✤✤✤✤

❖ GULAB JAMAM ❖

These are soft, light sponge balls, seeped in a delicate, flavoured syrup. Three or four pieces are more than enough for a portion and can be served warm or cold. You will need a deep frying pan or a Balti pan.

SERVES: 6-8

PREPARATION TIME: ABOUT 40 MINUTES

FOR THE SYRUP

450g (1lb) granulated sugar

600ml (1¼ pt) cold water

8 cardamom pods

FOR THE SPONGE BALLS

225g (8oz) full cream milk powder (or gulab jamam powder)

50g (2oz) self-raising flour

2.5ml (½tspn) ground cardamom

50g (2oz) melted butter or ghee

Cold milk to bind

About 600ml (1¼ pt) vegetable oil for deep-frying

1 Put the water, sugar and cardamom pods in a saucepan. Bring to the boil, stirring until the sugar has dissolved. Simmer, without stirring, for 15 minutes. Remove from the heat and discard the cardamom .

2 Sift the flour, milk powder and ground cardamom into a bowl. Stir in the melted butter and enough milk (about 150ml (¼pt)) to make a soft dough. Divide into about 30 portions and roll into balls.

3 Heat the oil in your pan. Test the heat by adding one ball of mix. It should rise to the surface after a few seconds and fry gently. If it colours very quickly, the oil is too hot. Adjust the temperature as necessary before cooking the remaining jamam in three or four batches, remembering that they will nearly double in size while cooking. Stir gently with a slotted spoon as they fry to ensure that they cook evenly. They should become a deep golden brown colour in 4-5 minutes.

4 Remove the jamam from the oil using the slotted spoon, drain and cool on kitchen paper for 5 minutes. Then transfer to the syrup. They will be quite delicate at this stage. Allow to cool completely.

5 This dessert can either be eaten cold or reheated gently in the syrup. Serve in individual dishes, making sure that each portion has plenty of syrup.

Cook's tip

As a special treat, add a dash of brandy or your favourite liqueur to the syrup before serving.

❖ CARROT HALVA ❖

This is probably one of the most popular Indian desserts and will not seem too unusual to those who have enjoyed carrot cake.

SERVES: 4

PREPARATION TIME: ABOUT 2 HOURS

450g (1lb) carrots

200g (7oz) granulated sugar

850ml (1½pt) full cream milk

50g (2oz) ghee or unsalted butter

25g (1oz) sultanas

2.5ml (½tspn) ground cardamom

25g (1oz) flaked almonds

10g (½oz) chopped unsalted pistachios

1 Peel and grate the carrots - a food processor earns its keep here - and place in a heavy based saucepan with the sugar and milk. Cook over a low heat for 1-1½ hours, stirring occasionally, until all the liquid has evaporated.

2 Add the ghee or butter and sultanas. Turn the heat to medium high and fry the carrot mixture, stirring continually to prevent the mix from sticking to the base of the pan. During this process, the carrots lose their wet, milky look and become a richer, darker colour. This will take 15-20 minutes. Remove the pan from the heat and stir in the cardamom. Mix well and turn into a serving dish.

3 Serve hot or cold, sprinkled with the almonds and pistachios.

♣ KHEER ♣

This exotic version of rice pudding is made with ground rather than pudding rice and can be served hot or cold. The basic recipe can be flavoured in many ways (see Cook's tip for Vermicelli Pudding on page 185) and can be made with sago or semolina for a change.

SERVES: 4-6

PREPARATION TIME: 1¼ HOURS

10g (½oz) ghee or unsalted butter

2.5ml (½tspn) ground cinnamon or nutmeg

110g (4oz) ground rice

1.25 litres (2pt) full cream milk

175g (6oz) granulated sugar

25g (1oz) sultanas

5ml (1tspn) ground cardamom

Blanched almonds to garnish

1 Melt the ghee or butter in a heavy based saucepan. Add the cinnamon and cook, stirring, for 30 seconds. Add the rice and half the milk and stir well. Cover the pan and cook for 15-20 minutes. Stir the mixture well and add the sugar and remaining milk. Simmer gently for 20 minutes, stirring frequently to prevent the rice from sticking to the base of the pan. The mixture should now be quite thick. If it is too thick, add a little more milk and cook for a further 5 minutes. Add the sultanas and check for sweetness.

2 Remove from the heat and stir in the cardamom. Pour the mixture into a serving dish and sprinkle with nuts. This dessert is particularly good if chilled in the refrigerator before serving.

♣ SEMOLINA AND ALMOND HALVA ♣

This halva is quick to make and delicious. As well as being served as a dessert, it can also be prepared as a sweetmeat to serve with coffee.

SERVES: 6-8

PREPARATION TIME: 15 MINUTES

175g (6oz) ghee or unsalted butter

175g (6oz) ground semolina

175g (6oz) caster sugar

175g (6oz) ground almonds

2.5ml (½tspn) ground nutmeg

2.5ml (½tspn) ground cardamom

425ml (¾pt) full cream milk

Flaked almonds to garnish

1 Grease a 20 x 30cm (8 x 12 inch) Swiss roll tin.

2 Melt the butter in a heavy based saucepan over a low heat. Add the semolina and cook, stirring, for 5–6 minutes or until the mixture turns golden brown. Remove from the heat.

3 Add the sugar, ground almonds and spices and mix in thoroughly. Add the milk a little at a time, stirring between additions, until a smooth paste is reached.

4 Return the saucepan to the heat and cook gently, stirring all the time, until the mixture thickens. Pour into the prepared tin, level the top, and sprinkle the almonds over the top. Press down slightly so that the almonds stick to the mixture. Allow to cool.

5 Cut into small squares to serve.

♣ BARFI ♣

Barfi is a kind of fudge made with gram flour. This is available in Asian stores and health food shops. It is made from ground gram lentils (chana), which resemble yellow split peas in colour and size.

MAKES: ABOUT 50 PIECES

PREPARATION TIME: 40-45 MINUTES

350g (12oz) ghee or unsalted butter

275g (10oz) gram flour, sifted

275ml (½pt) water

350g (12oz) granulated sugar

Pinch of salt

5ml (1tspn) ground cardamom

50g (2oz) flaked almonds

1 Grease a 20 x 30cm (8 x 12 inch) Swiss roll tin.

2 In a heavy based saucepan over a medium heat, melt the butter, add the gram flour, and cook for 5-6 minutes, stirring continuously, until the mixture is light brown. Remove from the heat. The flour must be cooked to avoid any raw flavour, but it does burn easily, so stir well and don't be tempted to speed up the process by turning up the heat.

3 In another saucepan, heat the sugar and water until the sugar is dissolved. Bring to the boil for about 5 minutes until the mixture is light golden. Don't stir, as this may cause the sugar to crystallise.

4 Add the gram flour mixture to the syrup and cook over a low heat for 10-15 minutes, stirring continuously, until the mixture leaves the sides of the pan and starts to form a ball.

5 Remove from the heat and stir in the cardamom, salt and nuts. Pour into the tray and smooth the surface.

6 Mark into diamonds or squares while still warm, and cut up when completely cold.

❖❖❖❖❖❖❖❖❖❖❖❖❖❖❖❖❖❖❖❖❖❖❖❖❖❖

Cook's tip

Vary this recipe by adding raisins, chopped glacé cherries or candied orange zest in place of the flaked almonds.

❖❖❖❖❖❖❖❖❖❖❖❖❖❖❖❖❖❖❖❖❖❖❖❖❖❖

♣ TROPICAL FRUIT SALAD ♣

Here is a classic dessert given an intriguing twist. You can, of course, vary the fruit selection and also make use of the wide variety of teas now readily available.

SERVES: 4

PREPARATION TIME: 1 HOUR

150ml (¼ pt) water

20ml (4tspn) loose tea leaves

2.5cm (1 inch) cube root ginger, grated (no need to peel)

110g (4oz) soft light brown sugar

150ml (¼pt) orange juice

5ml (1tspn) ground cardamom

A selection of prepared fresh fruit: mango, pineapple, guava, banana, apples, oranges, grapes, etc., cut into pieces and tossed in lemon juice

1 Place the water in the saucepan and bring to the boil. Add the tea, ginger and sugar, and stir until the sugar is dissolved. Leave for 10 minutes and then strain. Cool.

2 To the cooled liquid, add the orange juice and cardamom.

3 Place the fruit in a serving dish and pour the syrup over. Chill well. Serve with yoghurt or cream.

Cook's tip

A delicious, "store cupboard" version of this dish can be made using dried fruits. Strain the liquid at stage 1, return it to the saucepan and add a selection of ready soaked fruits: apricots, prunes, apple rings, pears etc. Simmer for 20 minutes, cool and proceed as above.

❧ MANGOES ❧

Mangoes are a delicious fruit, now readily available all year round in many supermarkets and greengrocers'. When buying fresh mangoes, look for those with a strong mango aroma and a clear yellow skin with a reddish flush. When squeezed they should yield slightly. To prolong shelf-life, mangoes are often put on sale before they are fully ripe, and these fruit will need to be ripened at home. Simply wrap each one in kitchen paper and store in a covered container in a warm room. Check them daily. Mangoes have a large flat stone, so slice down each side of the stone with a sharp knife, leaving two "halves" and a central piece with the stone in it. (You can cut a little more flesh away from this stone piece.)

An attractive way to serve the mango is to cut criss-cross slits deep into the cut flesh, but not through the skin, of each half. Push the fruit inside out and you will achieve a hedgehog effect.

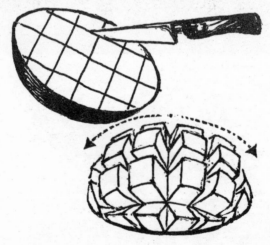

If you have mangoes that are rather over-ripe, make a luscious mango fool by scraping the flesh from the skin, mashing it with a fork and mixing it with an equal quantity of softly whipped double cream.

DRINKS

RECIPES

1 LASSI

A refreshing blend of yoghurt and water

2 AROMATIC FRUIT JUICE

A delicious way to spice up your favourite fruit juice, served hot or cold

3 ALMOND MILK DRINK

A delicious hot or cold drink with an unusual texture

4 MILKSHAKES

Deliciously creamy fruit drinks

PAPAYA

MANGO AND BANANA

5 SPICED TEA

An exciting twist on a national drink

6 CARDAMOM COFFEE

The perfect end to a Balti meal

Drinks
♦♦♦

The discussion about what should be drunk with a curry is a complex one. There is a school of thought that says that lager is the only accompaniment, and the hotter the curry and the more plentiful the lager, the better. Another argument would be that wine is wasted with spicy food and should never be drunk with an Indian or Balti meal. Others may say that most Indians and Pakistanis are teetotal, so no alcohol should be consumed. There is in fact a grain of truth in all these theories.

If you enjoy lager, and there is a wide range to choose from, then by all means drink it with your Balti. If you are feeling purist, you might wish to select an Indian lager, such as Cobra, but this is not essential. Certain red and white wines go exceptionally well with a curry and if the dish is delicately spiced, as many in this book are, then you can afford to be quite sophisticated in your choice of wine. And, of course, if you're feeling reckless and perhaps you are serving your Balti as a celebration, why not pop a bottle of champagne? Nothing vintage, and not too dry, but just about any eating occasion can be enhanced by a glass of fizz.

Only some faiths forbid alcohol, but there is an argument that says non-alcoholic drinks are more refreshing and certainly help to cleanse the palate between different dishes. In this chapter you will find a number of refreshing, non-alcoholic drinks to enjoy with your Balti, and why not end your meal with spiced tea or cardamom coffee?

Whatever you decide, remember that the idea is for you to enjoy your meal and there are no hard and fast rules. If this means that you sip a piña colada with your Balti, then so be it - they're your taste buds!

♣ LASSI ♣

This is a yoghurt-based drink often served with meals. It is a useful cooler with a particularly fiery curry and may be made sweet or savoury, depending on personal preference.

SERVES: 4

PREPARATION TIME: 5 MINUTES

SWEET LASSI

275ml (½pt) unsweetened natural yoghurt

50g (2oz) caster sugar (or to taste)

1 litre (1¾pt) ice cold water

Ice cubes, lemon slices and sprigs of mint to serve

Beat the yoghurt and sugar together thoroughly. Add the water and mix well. Pour into chilled tall glasses and top with ice cubes, a lemon slice and a sprig of mint.

SAVOURY LASSI

275ml (½pt) unsweetened natural yoghurt

2.5ml (½tspn) salt

Few twists of freshly ground black pepper

1 litre (1¾pt) ice cold water

Garnish as above

Make and garnish as sweet lassi, adding salt and pepper to taste.

❖ AROMATIC FRUIT JUICE ❖

This is a great way to turn your favourite fruit juice into a delicious drink that makes an excellent hot or cold accompaniment to a curry.

SERVES: 4

PREPARATION TIME: 5 MINUTES (+ COOLING TIME IF SERVING COLD)

1 litre (1¾pt) fruit juice (orange, pineapple, apple etc.)

4 cardamom pods

2 cloves

2.5cm (1 inch) stick of cinnamon

30ml (2tbspn) lemon juice

1 Place fruit juice, cardamom pods, cloves and cinnamon in a saucepan and heat gently over a medium heat for 5 minutes.

2 Remove from the heat and stir in the lemon juice. If serving hot, pour at once into heat-proof glasses. If serving cold, cool and chill in the refrigerator, before serving poured over ice in tall glasses.

♣ ALMOND MILK DRINK ♣

This drink has an unusual texture. It can be served ice cold, straight from the refrigerator, but also makes a soothing bedtime drink if served hot.

SERVES: 2

PREPARATION TIME: 5-10 MINUTES

570ml (1pt) full cream milk

40g (1½oz) ground almonds

10ml (2tspn) caster sugar

Pinch of cinnamon

Pinch of nutmeg

TO SERVE COLD

1 Mix all the ingredients together, stirring thoroughly to ensure the sugar is dissolved. Refrigerate.

2 Serve poured over ice in tall glasses.

TO SERVE HOT

1 Heat the milk in a pan over a high heat. When nearly boiling, stir in the sugar and dissolve. Add the almonds, cinnamon and nutmeg. Cover the pan, remove from the heat and leave for 2 minutes.

2 Stir and pour into two large mugs. Sprinkle with a little grated nutmeg, ground cinnamon or grated chocolate and serve at once.

❧ PAPAYA SHAKE ❧

You will need a liquidiser or food processor to make this delicious fruit drink.

SERVES: 4

PREPARATION TIME: 15 MINUTES

450g (1lb) ripe papaya, peeled, seeded and cut into chunks

10ml (2tspn) lemon juice

Pinch of cinnamon

150ml (¼pt) orange juice

10ml (2tspn) runny honey

275ml (½pt) full cream milk

Ice and cinnamon to serve

1 Put papaya, lemon juice, cinnamon and orange juice in a liquidiser or food processor and purée. Add the honey and milk and work until smooth.

2 Pour over the ice into tall glasses and sprinkle with a little extra cinnamon to serve.

♣ MANGO AND BANANA SHAKE ♣

This drink is simple to make and a great favourite with children.

SERVES: 4

PREPARATION TIME: 5 MINUTES

2 large bananas

1 large ripe mango

275ml (½pt) full cream milk

75ml (5tbspn) orange juice

Ice cubes

1 Remove all the flesh from the mango (see page 198) and chop roughly. Break the peeled bananas into pieces and place all the ingredients except the ice into a liquidiser or food processor and whiz together for about 1 minute until smooth.

2 Pour into tall glasses and add ice cubes to serve.

Cook's tip

Freshly picked mint leaves make an attractive garnish for this drink. Or you could sprinkle a little cinnamon on the top.

♣ SPICED TEA ♣

This unusual milk-based tea can be served at tea time or at the end of a meal. It has a particularly warming quality on cold winter days. Even if you normally do not take sugar in your tea, try this recipe - the sweetness can always be adjusted.

SERVES: 4

PREPARATION TIME: 15 MINUTES

570ml (1pt) full cream milk

150ml (¼pt) water

5cm (2 inch) stick of cinnamon, broken in two

10 cardamom pods

4 cloves

2 bay leaves

20-40ml (4-8tspn) sugar

4 tea bags

1 Place the milk, water, cinnamon, cardamom, cloves and bay leaves in a saucepan. Bring to the boil and simmer gently for 10 minutes.

2 Stir in the sugar to taste and mix until dissolved.

3 Add the tea bags, stir once, cover and remove from the heat. Allow to stand for 2-3 minutes.

3 Strain the tea into cups and serve at once.

♣ CARDAMOM COFFEE ♣

Coffee always tastes especially good after a spicy meal, and this version offers a delicately aromatic flavour.

SERVES: 8

PREPARATION TIME: 15 MINUTES

50g (2oz) ground coffee

7.5ml (1½tspn) ground cardamom, plus extra to sprinkle

25g (1oz) fresh ginger, grated

Milk or cream

Plain chocolate, grated

1 Mix the coffee with the ground cardamom and grated ginger, and make in your usual way - in a filter, cafetière, jug or percolator.

2 Pour into cups, add cream or milk if desired, and sprinkle with grated chocolate and cardamom.

A BALTI BANQUET

RECIPES

1 SPICY POTATO CHIPS

Delicious nibbles with pre-Balti drinks

2 SAMOSAS

Little pastry parcels with a variety of fillings

MEAT

VEGETABLE

3 SPICY NUTS

An unusual way to prepare favourite nibbles

4 TANDOORI LAMB CHOPS WITH MINT DIP

A simply delicious dish for any occasion

5 LAMB KEBABS

Spicy minced lamb served on skewers

6 MIXED VEGETABLE PAKORAS

These deep-fried parcels make a delicious starter

7 LENTIL SOUP

A hearty soup, perfect to begin a winter's meal

8 PARTY BALTI

A special meat Balti with a little of everything

9 VEGETARIAN PARTY BALTI

A delicious mixture of flavours that non-vegetarians will also find irresistible

10 FISH PARTY BALTI

The flavours of fresh, seasonal fish make this an excellent choice for a special occasion

10 KULFI WITH CHOCOLATE SAUCE AND ALMOND BISCUITS

Sheer indulgence!

11 LEMON SORBET

A refreshing end to a special Balti meal

By now you will have discovered that Baltis are so easy to cook that they make excellent everyday meals. But now that you are an accomplished Balti cook, you may want to display your talents to a wider audience - a Balti dinner party is just the thing.

A main-course Balti dish with one or two accompaniments or side dishes makes a hearty meal, as you know. A Balti party, however, gives you the opportunity to try some exciting starters, some very special Balti dishes and some refreshing desserts. Balti really is a great way to entertain. Invest in a Balti dish and stand for each of your guests and treat them to an evening of completely new culinary experiences!

Naturally it's wise to check that your friends enjoy spicy food before planning a Balti menu. Although you can vary the heat levels in all dishes, some people are strangely wary of anything that could be described as even slightly spicy.

On the following pages, you will find ideas for starters, main courses and desserts, and some suggested menus. Of course, if you have favourite recipes from elsewhere in this book, you can also use these. It is always wise to cook dishes you are comfortable with when entertaining - you'll feel much more relaxed to enjoy the company of your guests if you are not wondering at the back of your mind whether a new recipe will "work". Remember that most Balti dishes are quick to make and fun to cook. Why not invite your guests to join you in the kitchen? Provided with drinks and a few authentic nibbles, they will be fascinated to watch and you can all enjoy yourselves!

SAMPLE MEAT-BASED BALTI MENU

SPICY POTATO CHIPS

MEAT-FILLED SAMOSAS WITH CHUTNEY

TANDOORI LAMB CHOPS WITH MINT DIP

PARTY BALTI

VEGETABLE BALTI

PARATHAS

NAAN BREAD

TOMATO AND ONION SALAD

SPICY FRUITED CHUTNEY

KULFI

CHOCOLATE SAUCE

ALMOND BISCUITS

CARDAMOM COFFEE

BARFI

SAMPLE VEGETARIAN BALTI MENU

VEGETABLE-FILLED SAMOSAS WITH CHUTNEY

SPICY NUTS

MIXED VEGETABLE PAKORAS

CORIANDER CHUTNEY

VEGETARIAN PARTY BALTI

CHAPPATIS

NAAN BREAD

ONION AND CUCUMBER RAITA

APPLE AND APRICOT CHUTNEY

TROPICAL FRUIT SALAD

LEMON SORBET

SPICED TEA

SEMOLINA AND ALMOND HALVA

♣ SPICY POTATO CHIPS ♣

This is a delicious way to wake up your taste buds before a Balti meal. Don't make too many - guests abandon all discipline when tempted by these spicy nibbles.

PREPARATION TIME: 20 MINUTES

450g (1lb) potatoes, washed but not peeled

60ml (4tbspn) ghee or vegetable oil

4 cloves garlic, crushed

5ml (1tspn) cumin seeds

1 red chilli, finely chopped

1 green chilli, finely chopped

Salt

1 Cut the potatoes into very thin chips about 2.5cm (1 inch) long. Wash and dry thoroughly.

2 Heat the oil or ghee in a Balti pan, wok or deep frying pan over a medium heat. Add the garlic and cook for 5 minutes until golden brown.

3 Add the cumin seeds and chillies and cook for 2-3 minutes.

4 Add the chips and toss in the flavoured oil in the pan. Cover and fry gently for about 10 minutes, turning occasionally until the chips are tender.

5 Turn the heat up slightly, remove the lid and sizzle the chips for a further 2-3 minutes.

6 Remove from the pan with a slotted spoon, drain on kitchen paper and serve, sprinkled with a little salt.

♣ SAMOSAS ♣

Samosas are little pastry parcels, containing a variety of fillings - the choice is really up to you. I've included meat and vegetable samosas here. If you are serving these as pre-dinner nibbles, you will want to make them quite small. This is rather fiddly and time-consuming, but it is fine to make and deep fry them earlier in the day and reheat them in a hot oven when you are ready to serve them. Alternatively, they can be eaten cold. Made larger, they are delicious for picnics or lunch-boxes.

MAKES: 24 SAMOSAS

PREPARATION TIME: 1¼-1½ HOURS

225g (8oz) plain flour

Pinch of salt

45ml (3tbspn) vegetable oil

Hot water

MEAT FILLING

15ml (1tbspn) ghee or vegetable oil

1 medium onion, finely chopped

2 cloves garlic, crushed

1 green chilli, finely chopped

350g (12oz) minced meat - lamb, beef or chicken

15ml (1tbspn) fresh coriander, chopped

15ml (1tbspn) lemon juice

15ml (1tbspn) mango chutney

Salt

VEGETABLE FILLING

450g (1lb) potatoes, peeled and cut into 1cm (½ inch) cubes

75g (3oz) peas

30ml (2tbspn) ghee or vegetable oil

2.5ml (½tspn) cumin seeds

5ml (1tspn) Balti garam masala (see page 54)

2.5ml (½tspn) turmeric

1 green chilli, finely chopped

Salt

Vegetable oil for deep frying

TO MAKE THE PASTRY

1 Sieve together the flour and salt. Mix in the oil and add enough water to form a stiff dough.

2 Knead the dough for about 10 minutes until perfectly smooth.

TO MAKE THE MEAT FILLING

1 Heat the ghee or oil in a Balti pan, wok or frying pan over a medium heat. Add the onion, garlic and chilli and cook for 5-10 minutes until the onion is softened and golden.

2 Add the minced meat and a little water and fry gently for about 10 minutes, until the meat is cooked and the mix looks dry.

3 Stir in the coriander, lemon juice and mango chutney. Mix well, add salt to taste and allow to cool.

TO MAKE THE VEGETABLE FILLING

1 Heat the ghee or oil in a Balti pan, wok or frying pan over a medium heat. Add the cumin seeds and sizzle for a few seconds before adding the potatoes, peas, garam masala, turmeric and chilli.

2 Fry for 2-3 minutes, then add a little water, lower the heat, cover and cook for about 10 minutes or until potatoes are tender and the mix is fairly dry. Add salt to taste and allow to cool.

ASSEMBLING AND COOKING THE SAMOSAS:

1 Divide the dough into 12 balls. Roll out these balls on a very lightly floured board to give circles about 15cm (6 inches) in diameter. Cut these circles in half.

2 Pick up a semicircle and twist it round to form a cone. Brush the overlapping edges with a little water to seal them.

3 Fill the cone with about 7.5-10ml (1½-2tspn) of the filling of your choice, brush the top edges with a little water and twist over to seal.

4 Repeat this process with the remaining samosas - you'll find that you soon get the knack of filling them at speed.

5 Heat the oil in a Balti pan, wok or deep frying pan to give a depth of about 3cm (1¼ inches) of oil. Gently fry the samosas, about 6 at a time, until they become golden brown. You may need to turn them halfway through.

6 Drain the cooked samosas on kitchen paper.

7 Serve hot or cold with a chutney dip.

♣ SPICY NUTS ♣

This recipe provides an excellent alternative to the bowls of crisps and salted peanuts that usually appear with pre-dinner drinks. It is quick and easy to make and the nuts can be stored in an air-tight container for 2-3 weeks. You can use almost any kind of unsalted nuts - peanuts, cashews, hazelnuts, almonds, pistachios or a mixture.

MAKES: ABOUT 450G (1LB)

PREPARATION TIME: 20 MINUTES

425ml (¾pt) vegetable oil

450g (1lb) unsalted nuts

5ml (1tspn) salt

5ml (1tspn) ground black pepper

5ml (1tspn) chilli powder

2.5ml (½tspn) paprika

1 Heat the oil in a Balti pan, wok or deep frying pan over a high heat.

2 Add about a fifth of the nuts and fry until golden brown - about 20-30 seconds. Quickly lift them out on to kitchen paper using a slotted spoon or metal sieve. Repeat with the remaining nuts.

3 In a large bowl, blend the salt, pepper, chilli powder and paprika. Add the nuts and toss until well coated.

4 Serve either hot or cold.

♣ TANDOORI LAMB CHOPS WITH ♣ MINT DIP

This is quite simply a wonderful dish. Choose the most tender, meaty lamb cutlets you can find. Two chops per person should be plenty for a starter. Three chops and a green salad would be a delicious light lunch.

SERVES: 4

PREPARATION TIME: 15 MINUTES + 3 HOURS MARINATING

8 lamb cutlets

275ml (½pt) tandoori marinade (see page 59)

150ml (¼pt) natural yoghurt

30ml (2tbspn) fresh mint, chopped

1 clove garlic, crushed

Paprika

1 Arrange the cutlets in a single layer in a fairly shallow dish. Pour the marinade over the chops, turn them so that they are fully covered and leave the dish at room temperature for 3 hours.

2 Meanwhile, mix the chopped mint and crushed garlic into the yoghurt. Divide between 4 small dishes, sprinkle each one with a pinch of paprika and chill until required.

3 When the chops are fully marinated, heat your grill to its highest setting. Lift the cutlets out of the marinade, wiping off any excess. Wrap a piece of foil around the bare bone and arrange the cutlets on the grill rack.

4 Cook the cutlets for about 5 minutes on each side. They should begin to char around the edges.

5 Serve the cutlets with the dip.

♣ LAMB KEBABS ♣

These are a delicious blend of minced lamb, seasonings and spices, formed on to skewers and grilled. For a starter, you can make these as tiny kebabs, formed on cocktail sticks. Using a food processor, these kebabs can be whizzed together in no time.

SERVES: 4

PREPARATION TIME: 20 MINUTES

225g (8oz) lean lamb, minced quite finely

½ small onion, very finely chopped

2 green chillies, finely chopped

2.5cm (1 inch) cube fresh root ginger, grated

2 cloves garlic, crushed

5ml (1tspn) salt

5ml (1tspn) Balti spice mix (see page 53)

15ml (1tbspn) fresh coriander, chopped

A little beaten egg

1 Mix together the lamb, onion, chillies, ginger, garlic, salt, spices and coriander in a large bowl. Add enough beaten egg to make a slightly sticky mix that binds together well.

2 Divide the mix into 16 pieces, roll into small sausage shapes and push a cocktail stick through the length - a small piece of stick should remain uncovered as a handle.

3 Preheat the grill to medium-high. Arrange the kebabs on the rack and cook for about 10 minutes, turning occasionally until nicely browned. Serve with lemon wedges, a little green salad and any of the dips or chutneys mentioned in this book.

♣ MIXED VEGETABLE PAKORAS ♣

This is a popular snack that also makes an excellent starter when served with a chutney- or yoghurt-based dip. A mixture of vegetables is bound in a spicy, gram-flour batter and deep fried. As with so many recipes, the vegetables suggested are only a guide.

SERVES: 4

PREPARATION TIME: 40 MINUTES

1 clove garlic, crushed

2.5cm (1 inch) cube fresh root ginger, grated

2 green chillies, finely chopped

1 large onion, finely chopped

1 large potato, par-cooked until just tender and cut into small cubes

110g (4oz) frozen chopped spinach, defrosted and drained

175g (6oz) gram flour

10ml (2tspn) Balti spice mix (see page 53)

5ml (1tspn) turmeric

5ml (1tspn) salt

5ml (1tspn) cumin seeds

5ml (1tspn) crushed coriander seeds

15ml (1tbspn) fresh coriander, finely chopped

Vegetable oil for deep frying

1 Mix together the garlic, ginger, chillies, onion, potato and spinach.

2 Sieve the gram flour, spice mix, turmeric and salt into a large bowl. Add the cumin seeds, coriander seeds and fresh coriander. Mix with enough water to make a stiff batter and fold in the vegetables.

3 Heat the oil in a Balti pan, wok or deep frying pan to a depth of 3cm (1¼ inches) over a medium to high heat. Add 15ml (1tbspn) of the mixture to the oil, repeating until you have about 10 pieces. Cook for 3-4 minutes, until golden brown, turning halfway through.

4 Drain on kitchen paper and keep warm while cooking the remaining mix. Serve hot with lemon wedges to squeeze over and a little green salad as garnish.

Cook's tip

You can add diced, cooked meat or cooked fish if you wish.

✤ LENTIL SOUP ✤

A soup makes a good starter if your main course Balti is a dryish one. Because this soup is quite filling, you may wish to serve it on its own, without bread.

SERVES: 6

PREPARATION TIME: 35 MINUTES

45ml (3tbspn) ghee or vegetable oil

1 large onion, finely chopped

15ml (1tbspn) Balti garam masala

1 litre (1¾pt) vegetable or chicken stock

2 medium potatoes, peeled and cut into 1cm (½ inch) cubes

75g (3oz) red lentils

1 small green chilli, chopped

Salt

30ml (2tbspn) fresh coriander, chopped

1 Heat the ghee or oil in a Balti pan or large saucepan over a medium heat. Fry the onion until golden and softened and then add the garam masala and sizzle for a couple of minutes.

2 Add the stock, potato, lentils and chilli and simmer for about 30 minutes, until the lentils are cooked and the potato is tender.

3 Season to taste, stir in the coriander and serve.

✤ PARTY BALTI ✤

This dish has a little of everything! Ideal to serve at a dinner party, it combines chicken and lamb with vegetables, but you could try chicken and prawns or a single meat and more vegetables. Use any vegetables you like, remembering to choose some that will add colour to the dish.

SERVES: 6-8

PREPARATION TIME: 35 MINUTES

450g (1lb) par-cooked lamb (see page 104)

450g (1lb) chicken breast, cut into 2.5cm (1 inch) cubes

75ml (5tbspn) ghee or vegetable oil

3 large onions, finely chopped

6 cloves garlic, crushed

275ml (½pt) Balti sauce (see page 56)

30ml (2tbspn) Balti garam masala (see page 54)

30ml (2tbspn) fresh coriander, finely chopped

2 green peppers, cut into thin strips

1 red pepper, cut into thin strips

325g (11½oz) can sweetcorn, drained

15ml (1tbspn) natural Greek yoghurt

Fresh coriander leaves

1 Heat the ghee or oil in a Balti pan, wok or large frying pan over a medium heat. Add the onions and garlic and cook for about 10 minutes, until softened and golden brown.

2 Add the chicken pieces and cook for about 10 minutes until sealed and beginning to brown. Add the lamb and Balti sauce. Simmer for about 10 minutes.

225

3 Add the garam masala, chopped coriander, peppers and sweetcorn, and simmer for a further 10 minutes. Add a little water if the mixture seems too dry.

4 Check that the chicken is cooked and the lamb tender. The peppers should retain some of their crispness. Stir in a little more water if necessary - there should be some sauce.

5 Serve, topped with the yoghurt and garnished with coriander leaves.

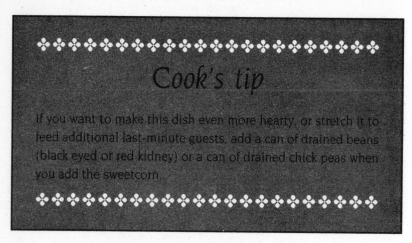

Cook's tip

If you want to make this dish even more hearty, or stretch it to feed additional last-minute guests, add a can of drained beans (black eyed or red kidney) or a can of drained chick peas when you add the sweetcorn.

✤ VEGETARIAN PARTY BALTI ✤

If you are not a vegetarian, you may fear that vegetarian food is bland and uninteresting - there's absolutely no danger of that with this vegetarian Balti! Balti cookery ensures that vegetables are not only spicy and full of flavour but also lightly cooked so that they retain their crispness and colour.

SERVES: 6-8

PREPARATION TIME: 45 MINUTES

45ml (3tbspn) ghee or vegetable oil

5ml (1tspn) cumin seeds

5ml (1tspn) mustard seeds

2 large onions, finely chopped

4 cloves garlic, crushed

30ml (2tbspn) Balti garam masala (see page 54)

2 green chillies, finely chopped

175g (6oz) courgettes, cut into 5mm ('/4 inch) slices

2 large potatoes

1 small cauliflower, cut into small florets

175g (6oz) mangetout, cut in half

175g (6oz) carrots, cut into matchsticks or thinly sliced

400g (14oz) can red kidney beans, drained

400g (14oz) can chopped tomatoes

325g (11'/2oz) can sweetcorn, drained

275ml ('/2pt) Balti sauce (see page 56)

15ml (1tbspn) fresh coriander, roughly chopped

150ml ('/4pt) natural Greek yoghurt

15ml (1tbspn) flaked almonds, toasted

227

1 Boil the potatoes until just tender. When cool enough to handle, cut into 1cm ('/₂ inch) cubes. You can leave the skin on, but it will probably peel off when you cut up the potatoes.

2 Lightly cook the cauliflower and carrots until just tender.

3 Heat the ghee or oil in a Balti pan, wok or large frying pan over a medium heat. Add the cumin and mustard seeds and sizzle for a few seconds. Then add the onion and garlic and cook for about 10 minutes, until the onion is golden brown and softened.

4 Add the Balti garam masala and green chillies and cook for a further 2-3 minutes, stirring all the time.

5 Add the mangetout and courgettes and stir fry for about 5 minutes, until they are beginning to soften.

6 Add the pre-cooked potatoes, cauliflower and carrots and the red kidney beans, tomatoes, sweetcorn and Balti sauce.

7 Simmer together for about 10 minutes until the vegetables are cooked to your taste, adding a little water if the mix seems too dry.

8 Stir in the coriander, and top with yoghurt and almonds to serve.

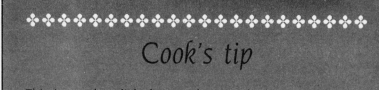

Cook's tip

This is another dish that can be stretched to accommodate unexpected guests. Simply increase the quantities of the "bulkier" ingredients - another potato or more red kidney beans. You may need to add more liquid, either another can of tomatoes or some water and tomato purée, and a little more spice mix or Balti sauce.

✦ FISH PARTY BALTI ✦

These days many people are trying to cut back on the amount of red meat they eat. Fish is therefore an obvious choice. In this recipe, the fish is marinated prior to cooking to enhance its flavour. Remember, fish needs no par-cooking and only a short cooking time.

SERVES: 6-8

PREPARATION TIME: 40 MINUTES + 2 HOURS MARINATING TIME

MARINADE

3 cloves garlic, peeled

1 small onion, peeled

30ml (2tbspn) coconut milk powder

15ml (1tbspn) vegetable oil

5ml (1tspn) Balti spice mix (see page 53)

1 green chilli

15ml (1tbspn) tomato purée

2.5cm (1 inch) cube fresh root ginger, grated

15ml (1tbspn) lemon juice

BALTI

450g (1lb) white fish fillets (e.g. cod or hake)

225g (8oz) salmon fillets

225g (8oz) peeled prawns

110g (4oz) shelled mussels

30ml (2tbspn) ghee or vegetable oil

3 cloves garlic. crushed

1 large onion, finely chopped

10ml (2tspn) Balti spice mix (see page 53)

2.5ml (½tspn) turmeric

2.5ml (½tspn) cumin seeds

275ml (½pt) Balti sauce (see page 56)

150ml (¼pt) double cream

60ml (4tbspn) natural yoghurt

75g (3oz) ground almonds

3 tomatoes, peeled and cut into 5mm (¼ inch) cubes

30ml (2tbspn) fresh coriander, roughly chopped

A few prawns in their shells

Sprig of fresh coriander

15ml (1tbspn) toasted flaked almonds

1 Mix together the ingredients for the marinade in a food processor or liquidiser with enough water to make a fairly thick pouring paste - about the consistency of tomato ketchup or salad cream. You can also pound the ingredients together using a pestle and mortar, first chopping the onion and chilli, and crushing the garlic.

2 Cut the white fish and salmon fillets into approximately 2.5cm (1 inch) cubes. Place the fish in the marinade, stirring the pieces carefully to make sure that all are coated. Cover the bowl and refrigerate for 2-4 hours.

3 Heat the ghee or oil in a Balti pan, wok or large frying pan over a medium heat. Add the garlic and onion and cook for 10 minutes until soft and golden.

4 Add the spice mix, turmeric and cumin seeds and cook, stirring, for 2 minutes.

5 Add the fish and marinade and cook gently for 2 minutes.

6 Add the Balti sauce, cream, yoghurt and almonds and simmer for about 15 minutes until the fish is just cooked. Stir carefully to avoid breaking the fish and add water if the dish is becoming too dry.

7 Stir in the tomatoes and chopped coriander and heat through for a further 3-4 minutes.

8 Serve, sprinkled with flaked almonds and garnished with the shell-on prawns and coriander sprig.

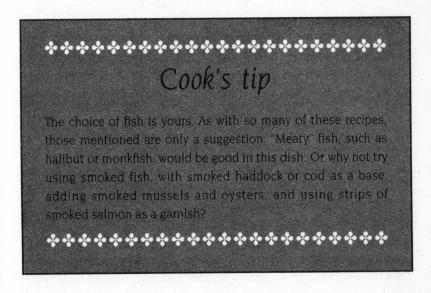

Cook's tip

The choice of fish is yours. As with so many of these recipes, those mentioned are only a suggestion. "Meaty" fish, such as halibut or monkfish, would be good in this dish. Or why not try using smoked fish, with smoked haddock or cod as a base, adding smoked mussels and oysters, and using strips of smoked salmon as a garnish?

♣ KULFI WITH CHOCOLATE SAUCE ♣ AND ALMOND BISCUITS

Kulfi (see page 186) is delicious on its own, but served with chocolate sauce and almond biscuits it is very special indeed. Although this is not an authentic Baltistani serving suggestion, I don't think you will hear your guests complaining! Of course, you can make the biscuits ahead of time and keep them in an air-tight tin. The chocolate sauce is quick to make just before serving.

SERVES: 6

PREPARATION TIME: 25 MINUTES (ASSUMING KULFI IS ALREADY MADE)

ALMOND BISCUITS

75g (3oz) butter

75g (3oz) caster sugar

50g (2oz) plain flour

75g (3oz) flaked almonds

1 Cream the butter and sugar together until light and fluffy. Stir in the flour and almonds and mix well.

2 Drop small spoonfuls of the mixture on to greased baking trays, allowing plenty of room for the biscuits to spread. Flatten with a damp fork.

3 Bake at 200°C/400°F/Gas Mark 6 for 6-8 minutes until the biscuits are pale golden. Leave them on the tray for one minute. Then carefully lift each biscuit off with a palette knife and press it over a greased rolling pin. As the biscuits cool, they will set hard in an attractive curved shape.

4 When set hard, remove the biscuits to a cooling rack until quite cold.

CHOCOLATE SAUCE

175g (6oz) good quality plain chocolate

25g (1oz) unsalted butter

25g (1oz) soft brown sugar

15ml (1tbspn) lemon juice

30ml (2tbspn) double cream

1 Break the chocolate into pieces and place in a small saucepan. Add the other ingredients and heat very gently until the chocolate has melted.

2 Bring to the boil and simmer for 1 minute, stirring all the time.

3 Serve the kulfi with the hot sauce poured over, accompanied by the biscuits.

♣ LEMON SORBET ♣

You can make this sorbet well in advance - it is always a useful stand-by in the freezer. The recipe includes single cream, which gives it a richer flavour and texture than some more traditional recipes. It also lacks the bitter taste that sorbets made with lemon zest can have.

SERVES: 6-8

PREPARATION TIME: 30-40 MINUTES + FREEZING TIME

150g (5oz) granulated sugar

Pinch of salt

215ml (7½ fl oz) water

150ml (¼pt) single cream

Juice of 4-5 large lemons - about 150ml (¼pt)

2 egg whites

40g (1½oz) caster sugar

1 Place the granulated sugar, salt and water in a large saucepan. Bring to the boil, stirring, and simmer for 5 minutes. Set aside to cool.

2 When the mixture is completely cool, add the cream and then the lemon juice, pour into a plastic tray (a large margarine tub is fine) and freeze until firm.

3 Beat the egg whites until almost firm, then gradually beat in all the caster sugar until the mixture stands in stiff peaks.

4 Break up the frozen mixture with a wooden spoon. Turn it into a bowl and beat it until smooth. A hand-held electric whisk used at low speed is ideal for this. Fold in the egg-white mixture and return quickly to a cold tray.

5. Freeze until firm and serve with fruit salad.

CURRY IN A HURRY

█ f you have just flicked through this book, you may now have the idea that Balti cookery is complicated and far too much effort. I hope that you will be able to find time to read the book thoroughly and realise that, taken a stage at a time, Balti is a very simple and relaxed form of cooking. You will also find, in many of the recipes I have included, time-saving tips. In this section, I have gathered together all these ideas for speeding up the Balti process and added a few more. Almost certainly, as you become a proficient Balti cook, you will discover labour- and time-saving tips of your own.

It is worth repeating that one of the easiest ways to save time is to read this book thoroughly. You need to have an idea of what Balti is about and how everything is pieced together before you can begin to find short-cuts for some of the recipes.

On the following pages, I will list some of the areas where I believe that time can be saved without spoiling the finished dish and also warn against some short-cuts that are simply not worth taking.

SPICES

We all know that spices are best bought whole, lovingly roasted and carefully ground to retain their freshness and release their flavours. The same is true of coffee, but most of us manage with instant a great deal of the time. It is not the end of the world if you resort to buying ready-ground spices.

Two recipes for garam masala are offered in this book. One uses whole spices, the other, much quicker option, blends ready-ground spices. The third option is to use a pre-prepared garam masala. The problem here is two-fold. Firstly, even if there is quite a detailed list of ingredients on the jar or tin, you will not know the exact proportions that have been used. Secondly, you do not know how long ago the mix was made. I suggest that you use this option only as a last resort.

236

If you are buying ready-ground spices, then a busy supermarket is your best option. It will have a fairly quick turn-around of stock, so your spices should be quite fresh. A final way to save time with spices is to make plenty of spice mix yourself. It is just as quick to weigh out 200g of a spice as it is to weigh out 20g. Store the mix in a sealed jar in a dark cupboard and use it as quickly as possible. Again, only use this short-cut if you will be cooking Baltis quite often.

BREADS

There are two time-saving options available. The first is to buy ready-made naan bread and chappatis. You may not find a very wide range of breads on the supermarket shelves, but what are there are excellent. Follow the reheating instructions on the pack exactly and you really can't go wrong.

The other choice is the packet-mix breads now available. These are basically "just-add-water" mixes. In fact, most Indian breads are basically a mix of flour and water anyway, so you are paying quite a lot for the added seasoning. Naan bread mixes are better value for money as they do away with the need to prove the dough.

CANNED PULSES AND LEGUMES

As I have mentioned elsewhere, I am inclined to feel that there are better things to do in the kitchen than boiling chick peas for hours. Especially when a few seconds with a tin-opener achieves a very similar result! It is true, of course, that boiling your own dried peas, beans and lentils is considerably cheaper, especially if you cook in bulk and freeze in batches. (A preserving pan is useful for cooking several pounds at once.) But you do have to allow time to soak and cook before you require your legumes and such planning is not always possible. For those of us blessed with less foresight, canned red kidney beans, black eyed beans, chick peas, lentils and sweetcorn are all perfectly acceptable for any of the recipes in which these ingredients are required.

PASTES AND SAUCES

Balti is the flavour of the moment and to prove it there are a number of ready-made Balti pastes and sauces now on the market. Of course, new ones are being brought out all the time and some of these may be acceptable to you, but on the whole I think that you will be disappointed by the results of your cooking if you use a ready-made sauce.

Ready-made Balti pastes are essentially mixtures of oil, spices, ginger and garlic plus a lot of acidic ingredients for preservation. If you wish to use these pastes, consider them as a replacement for the garlic, ginger and spices mentioned in the individual recipes.

Balti sauces are more complex. They are designed to be added to the fried meat and vegetables of your choice and come in a range of heat levels from mild to hot. If you really want to try such a sauce, I would suggest that you increase the amounts of onion, garlic and fresh ginger in your recipe, add the meat and vegetables and then add the sauce. When you are ready to serve, I would recommend the addition of lashings of freshly chopped coriander.

BALTI MEAT AND POULTRY

The par-cooking of meat for a Balti is so straightforward that there is really no way to speed up the process. However, time can be saved by doubling the recipe and freezing half. It is then ready for you next time you wish to cook a Balti.

The ingredient list for tandoori chicken is a little daunting, as is the time required for marination. If you are making a recipe incorporating tandoori meat, you could try a commercially produced variety. Most supermarkets have their own recipe, usually on light and dark chicken meat, and I suggest that you try several to find the one you prefer. However, if your dish relies totally on the tandoori marinade for its flavour, as with the tandoori lamb chops on page 220, then the time spent making the sauce and marinating the meat is really worthwhile.

A surprisingly successful short-cut when making Balti meat balls (see page 112) is to try using little cocktail sausages instead of the meat mix. You may need to spice up the sauce a little, but it works well and is very popular with children.

RELISHES

Although it is lovely to be able to produce a range of home-made chutneys to serve with your Balti, there is a huge variety available "off the shelf" and on the whole they are very good. Mango chutney in particular is really not worth making yourself, unless you stumble upon a glut of cheap mangoes. The choice on the supermarket shelf, however, is amazing. They range from mild to spicy and some include other flavours, such as lime or ginger. It is really trial and error to find the one you like best. Garlic chutney and lime pickle are my other supermarket favourites.

SNACKS AND STARTERS

The delicatessen counter at your supermarket will probably have samosas, pakoras and onion bhajis. You can be forgiven for buying these ready-made if you are a little wary of deep-fat frying or if you are putting all your energies into your Balti main course! Bombay mix is, of course, available everywhere and is a very acceptable pre-dinner nibble.

DESSERTS

You may be lucky enough to live near a specialist Asian shop selling ready-made desserts, but in many parts of the country these are few and far between. You can save time when making kulfi (see page 186) by replacing the boiled-down milk with condensed milk. The resulting ice-cream will be sweeter than if you boil down milk, but if you are planning to smother it with chocolate sauce (see page 233), then this is not a major problem!

Canned fruits have already been mentioned as being of good quality - mangoes in particular survive the canning process well. A can of mangoes in syrup makes an excellent basis for a fruit salad. Simply tip into a bowl, add chopped-up bananas and apples, grapes and a can of pineapple chunks in natural juice. Chill well for a quick and refreshing dessert.

MAIN MEALS

I discovered the following dish by accident but it's a real find. It takes no time to prepare, provided you have a jar of Balti spice mix to hand, and it tastes surprisingly good. It assumes that you have recently enjoyed a Sunday roast and, as I normally do, cooked far too many vegetables. This means that on Monday your refrigerator is crowded with the remains of a joint, the leftover vegetables, and some congealed gravy. Fear not! Cut the meat into 2cm (¾ inch) cubes, discarding any bones. Chicken, turkey, beef, pork, lamb and even gammon, if not too heavily cured, are fine for this. Cut the vegetables into evenly sized pieces. Then heat a little oil in a pan, add a chopped-up onion and a crushed garlic clove and sizzle for about 10 minutes. Add about 15ml (1tbspn) of Balti spice mix (see page 53) and cook for a couple of minutes. Add the meat, vegetables and gravy and simmer together for about 10 minutes until heated through. Serve with naan bread (cold Yorkshire puddings don't really work!). A sprinkling of freshly chopped coriander would be good but is not essential. This recipe is ideal for using up what you have, but a rough guide to proportions might be as follows:

For 4 people: 450g (1lb) cooked meat

                        450g (1lb) mixed cooked vegetables

                        150-275ml (¼-½pt) cold gravy

If you don't have any gravy, a tin of chopped tomatoes makes a good substitute.

USEFUL
INFORMATION

ADDRESSES

The Curry Club
PO Box 7
Haslemere
Surrey
GU27 1EP

For specialist ingredients and
equipment

The Balti House Kitchen
PO Box 4401
Henley-on-Thames
Oxfordshire
RG9 1FW

For specialist ingredients and
equipment

Divertimenti
139-141 Fulham Road
London
SW3

For general kitchen equipment

Lakeland Plastics Ltd
Alexandra Buildings
Windermere
Cumbria
LA23 1BQ

Particularly useful for freezer
equipment: tubs, labels, bags etc.
Because of its strong flavours, it is
useful to keep separate freezer
containers for your Balti dishes.

Loch Fyne Oysters
Clachan Farm
Cairndow
Argyll
PA26 8BH
Scotland

Fresh and smoked shellfish and fish, also fresh game.

Pinneys of Orford
Market Square
Orford
Woodbridge
Suffolk
IP12 2LH

Smoked fish and shellfish

Brown and Forrest
Thorney
Langport
Somerset
TA10 0DR

Smoked fish

Carew Oysters
Tything Barn
West Williamson
Carew
Kilgetty
Dyfed
SA68 0TN

Shellfish farm where oysters are grown, purified and packed

Suffolk Herbs
Sawyers Farm
Little Cornard
Sudbury
Suffolk
CO10 0NY

For herb seeds and plants, including coriander

GLOSSARY

Most recipes and ingredients in this book are referred to by English names, but you may well find it useful, when buying ingredients or navigating a Balti-house menu, to know the authentic terms. These words are from Hindi and Urdu, which are not written with the English alphabet, so you may see different spellings on menus or packaging.

Achar Pickle

Adrak Fresh ginger

Aloo Potato

Am Mango

Atta Wholewheat flour used to make chappatis

Badain Star anise

Badam Almond

Bargar Frying spices in hot oil to release their aromatic flavours

Besan A fine flour made from ground chana dal (similar to yellow split peas) used to make pakoras

Bhaji A mild vegetable curry, usually fairly dry

Bhuna Sizzling a spice paste in hot oil before other ingredients are added

Bindi Okra or ladies' fingers

Brinjal Aubergine or egg plant

Barfi A fudgy sweetmeat made from milk and often flavoured with cardamom, almond or pistachio

Chana dal A type of lentil, similar to yellow split peas

Chappati A flat, unleavened bread served hot with meat and vegetable dishes

Dahi Yoghurt

Dalchini Cinnamon

Dal (dhal) Lentils - a wide variety are used in Indian and Pakistani cooking

Dhania Coriander

Dhansak A Parsee dish usually containing tomatoes, lentils, aubergine and spinach

Elaichi Cardamom

Gajar Carrot

Galangal A rhizome similar to ginger. The latter is often used in its place in recipes, as it is hard to find except in very specialist shops

Garam masala Literally "hot mixture". A blend of spices used in cooking and to sprinkle as seasoning on finished dishes

Ghee Clarified butter, which can be heated to a higher temperature than butter in which milk solids are still present

Gobi Cauliflower

Gosht The word often translated as "meat" on Indian menus, this is usually lamb, mutton or goat on the Indian sub-continent

Gulab jamam Small balls of sponge deep-fried and served in a flavoured syrup

Halva A sweetmeat made by boiling sugar and fruit or vegetables until reduced and sticky. When cool it becomes firm and can be cut into small squares to serve. Carrot, pistachio and almond are popular flavours.

Huldi Turmeric

Jaifal Nutmeg

Jalfrezi A stir-fried meat dish usually containing green peppers and onions

Jeera Cumin

Jinga Prawns

Kabli chana Chick peas

Kala jeera Black cumin seeds

Karahi A round pan with two handles used for both cooking and serving food. Also known as a Balti pan

Kebab Meat on a skewer, usually cooked over charcoal

Keema A spiced dish made with minced meat

Kish mish Sultanas

Kofta Meatballs, usually deep-fried and served in a sauce

Korma A rich curry usually containing chicken, meat or vegetables cooked in a cream and yoghurt sauce.

Kulfi Ice-cream

Lassi A sweet (namkeen) or savoury (meethi) drink made of yoghurt

Lavang Cloves

Macchi Fish

Malai Cream

Masala Literally "a mixture", usually of spices

Masoor Red lentils

Mattar Green peas

Meethi Sweet

Methi Fenugreek

Mirch Pepper or chilli

Murgh Chicken

Namak Salt

Naan Teardrop-shaped leavened bread cooked in a tandoor and served hot with meat and vegetable dishes

Naryal Coconut

Nimboo Lime or lemon

Pakoras Mixtures of meat or vegetables deep-fried in batter

Palak Spinach

Poppadom Crispy pancake made of lentil flour, sometimes flavoured with garlic or spices

Paratha Deep-fried bread

Piaz Onion

Pista magaz Pistachio nut

Puri A deep-fried unleavened bread served hot with meat and vegetable dishes

Rai Mustard seeds

Raita A cool chutney of yoghurt and vegetables served with meat or vegetable dishes

Rajma Red kidney beans

Rogan josh Literally "red meat" or meat in a red sauce. The redness usually comes from paprika and tomatoes

Roti Bread

Sabji Vegetables

Sag Spinach

Sambals Little dishes containing accompaniments to a main meal

Sheek Skewer

Tandoori A term used to describe meat marinated in yoghurt and spices and cooked in a tandoor. Tandoori usually descibes meat cooked on the bone

Tikka As tandoori but removed from the bone and cut into smaller pieces

INDEX

Indvidual ingredients of recipes are not included in this index unless they are discussed in the introductory texts or Cook's tips. Entries in *italic type* are recipes.